AF521617

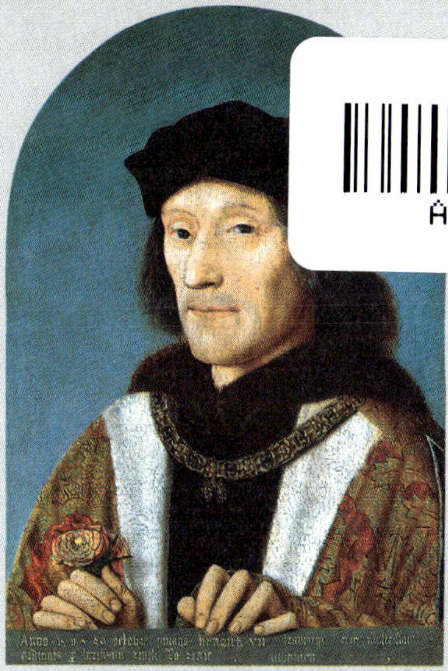

THE NATIONAL PORTRAIT GALLERY BOOK OF

THE TUDORS

Clare Gittings

SCALA

Sir Thomas More, his Father, his Household and his Descendants
Rowland Lockey, 1593, after Hans Holbein the Younger

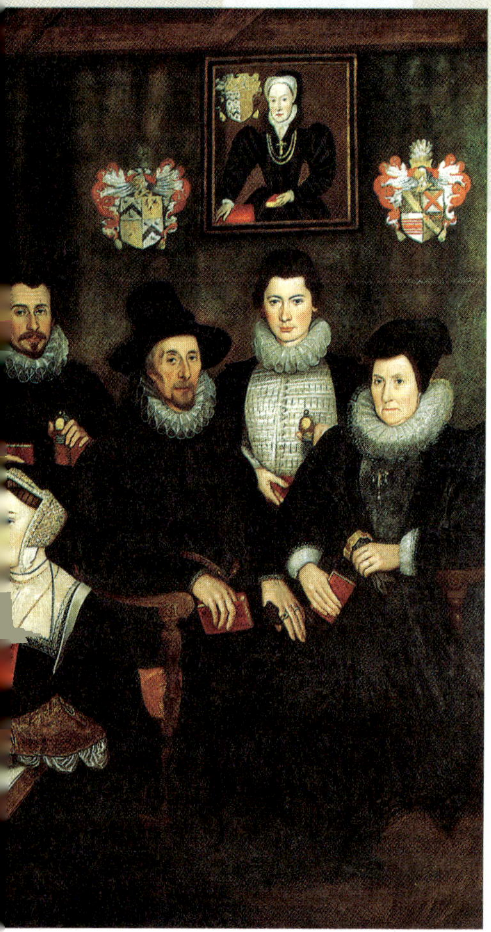

This portrait shows five generatior of the More family, grouped aroun its most famous member, Sir Thom More (1478–1535). Their lives spanned 200 years, from Sir John More (1451?–1530) on the left-hand side, a judge and the father of Thomas, to Thomas's youngest great-grandson and biographer Cresacre More (1572–1649), standing between his parents to the righ of the painting. A large painting of Sir Thomas More's family was the most ambitious work painted by Holbein during his first visit to England between 1526 and 1528. It was unfortunately destroyed in the eighteenth century, but variou copies have survived. This version by Rowland Lockey includes Elizabethan descendants of Thomas More.

More's unshakeable adherenc to Roman Catholicism clashed wit Henry VIII's more secular ambition Thomas had been Lord Chancellor,

The Foundation of the Tudors

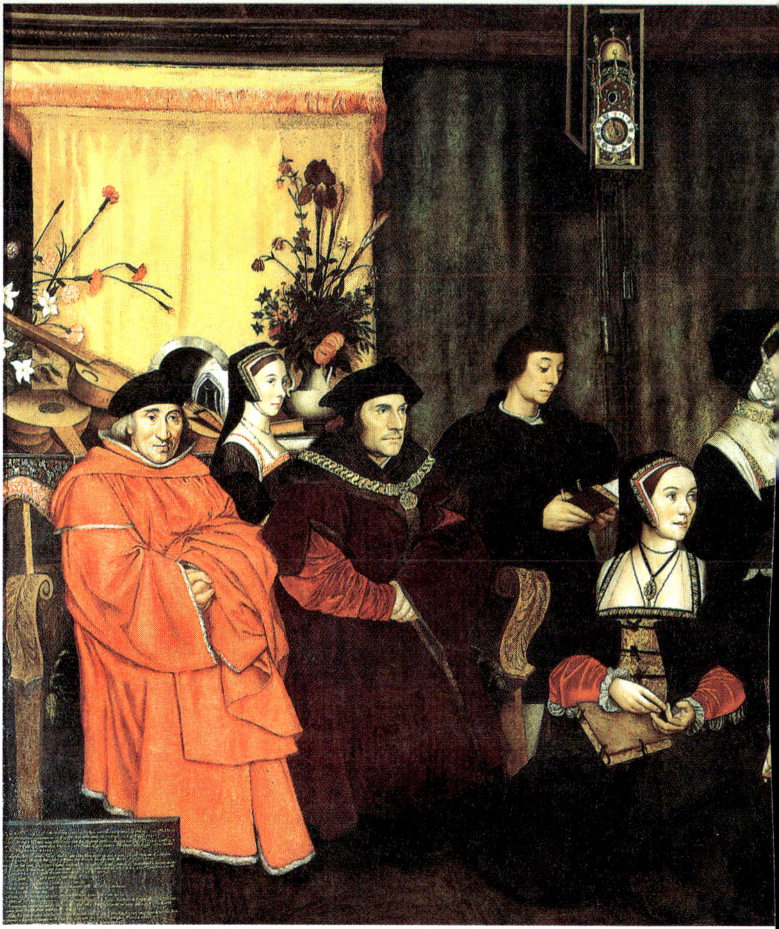

Introduction

This book presents the varying images of the immensely successful Tudor dynasty (1485–1603). It includes portraits not only of the monarchs but also of some of their spouses, courtiers, servants, enemies and friends. England around the year 1600 was a very different place from how it had been a century earlier. During this century of Tudor rule, England moved from being a small part of Catholic Christendom under the spiritual rule of the papacy, to a Protestant country with the monarch as head of the Church. There was also a huge shift in wealth away from the Church to the landowners, brought about by the dissolution of the monasteries. England became a country largely at peace with itself as the thirty years of intermittent fighting between the Yorkist and Lancastrian factions, known as the Wars of the Roses (1455–85), became a distant memory. Five Tudor monarchs ruled England during this period, from Henry VII, the founder of the dynasty (*reigned* 1485–1509) to Elizabeth I (*reigned* 1558–1603), perhaps the greatest Tudor ruler. Between them came the reigns of the forceful Henry VIII (1509–47) and his two most deeply religious children, the Protestant Edward VI (1547–53) and Catholic Mary I (1553–58).

The art of Tudor England, and in particular the painting of portraits, was greatly stimulated by religious controversies abroad. Foreign artists fled to a more peaceful England to escape persecution for their beliefs or to seek new markets when the demand for religious paintings diminished in their own countries. Finest among these painters was Hans Holbein the Younger, who visited England twice during the reign of Henry VIII. On his first visit he lived in the household of Sir Thomas More; during the second, he became painter to the king, dying in England in 1543. Holbein's sophisticated and vivid portraits dominated English Court taste from 1532. It has been calculated that one-fifth of all the nobility of Henry VIII's time sat to Holbein. In the second half of the century further refugee artists came to England, but Elizabeth's reign also saw the development of the more home-grown art of miniature painting, whose finest exponent was an Englishman, Nicholas Hilliard.

This book begins and ends with a painting of a Tudor family, one Catholic, the other Protestant. Examining how the two families met and responded to the challenges of the times gives an invaluable insight into the nature of the very great changes that took place during the century of Tudor rule.

King Henry VIII and his Image

It was during the reign of Henry VIII that some of the most far-reaching and lasting changes occurred, in particular the break from Rome and the dissolution of the monasteries, thus altering the political and economic face of Tudor England. In his policies Henry was ably served by his two greatest ministers, Cardinal Wolsey and Thomas Cromwell, though neither could save themselves from the king's wrath when they fell from power. Abroad, Henry was competing in magnificence with the King of France and the Holy Roman Emperor, but he was also desperate to prevent them from forming an alliance with each other against him. Weaving through all of this were Henry's matrimonial troubles and his need for a male heir to secure the Tudor dynasty. In projecting the desired image of himself, Henry was fortunate enough to attain the services of Hans Holbein the Younger, who for ten years created portraits of the monarch and his court that are unsurpassed in British history.

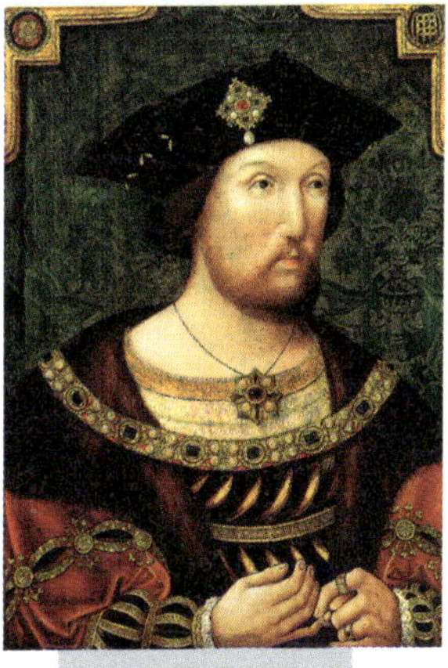

King Henry VIII
Unknown artist,
c. 1520

In this early painting by an unknown artist, Henry (1491–1547) had been on the throne for about a decade. Looking at those images of King Henry VIII that are not the work of Hans Holbein the Younger makes us realise just what a magnificent job Holbein later did for Henry, akin to a highly successful advertising campaign today. Henry was always very concerned about the impact of his image not just in England but elsewhere in Europe too, and was acutely aware of his powerful rivals abroad. An Italian writing in 1519 made a telling observation about the king's looks: 'He was very fair and his whole frame admirably proportioned. Hearing that King Francis [of France] wore a beard, he allowed his to grow, and as it was reddish, he had then got a beard which looks like gold.' The beard was to remain with Henry throughout his life, even if it became somewhat less golden by the end.

The Whitehall Mural,
King Henry VIII;
King Henry VII;
Elizabeth of York;
Jane Seymour
George Vertue, 1737, after Remigius van Leemput, after Hans Holbein the Younger

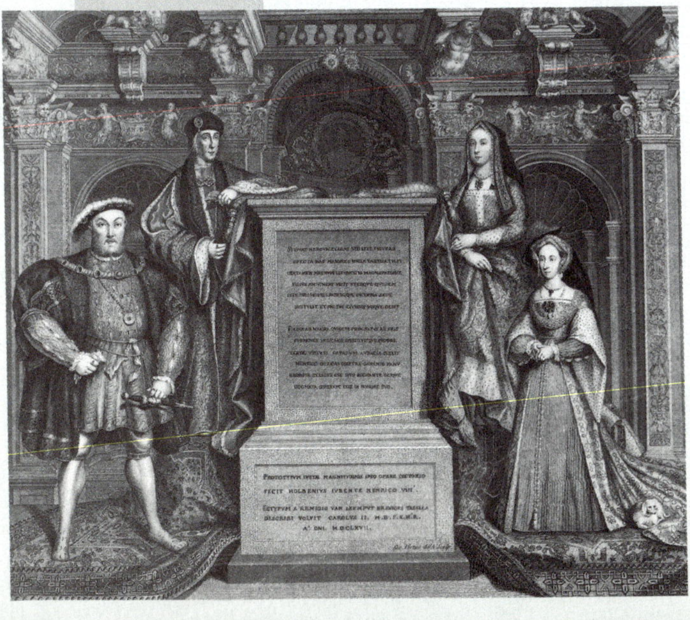

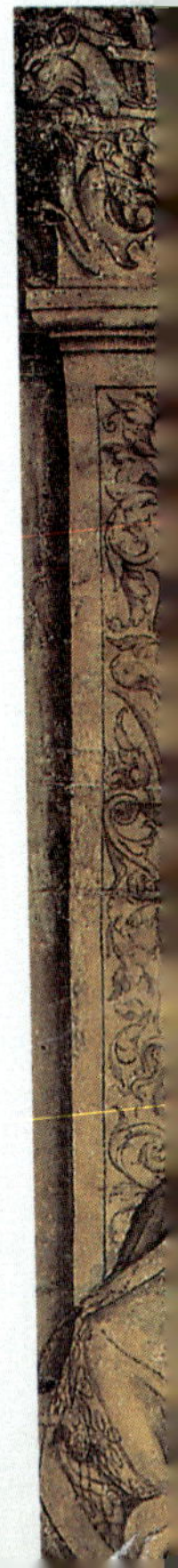

King Henry VII
Unknown artist,
1505

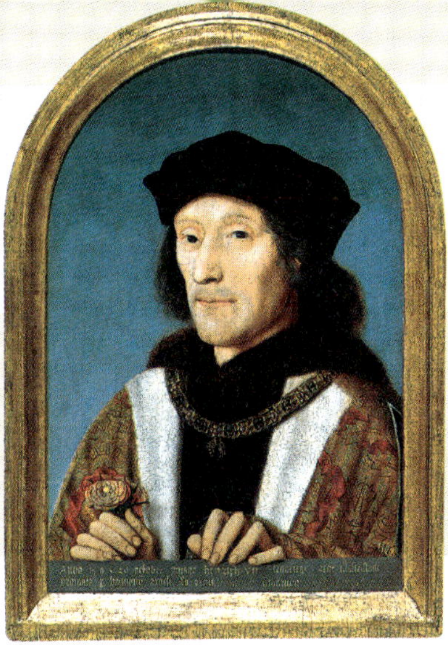

key minister at Henry's court, and a personal friend of the monarch. However he gave up his Chancellorship on principle over the relaxation of the heresy laws. As Henry's relations with the Pope deteriorated so Thomas's position as a faithful Roman Catholic became increasingly difficult. He refused to take the oath, under the Act of Supremacy, to make Henry head of the English Church, and was executed in 1535, declaring that he was 'the king's good servant, but God's first'.

In 1593 his grandson, also called Thomas More (1531–1606), had this painting made. The Elizabethan More family are easily identifiable by the ruffs around their necks. The later Thomas More faced heavy fines for his family's continuing Catholicism. Sitting wearing a high hat, he dominates the right-hand side of the painting, just as his famous grandfather does the left.

This is an unusually realistic and unflattering portrait of Henry VII (1457–1509) because of the role it played in the negotiations for a possible marriage. After Elizabeth of York's death, Henry VII considered taking as his second wife Margaret of Austria, the daughter of the Holy Roman Emperor Maxmilian I. This picture, by Margaret's own Court painter, was commissioned by the Emperor's agent. Henry was therefore less able to control how he was portrayed than if the artist had been working directly for him. The inscription records the date of the sitting, 20 October 1505, making this the oldest painting in the National Portrait Gallery's collection. The

As painter to Henry VIII, Holbein's most important task was to present the monarch as a mighty Renaissance prince. From about 1536 to 1537 he did this by producing a magnificent wall painting for the Privy Chamber of Whitehall Palace in London. Henry VIII was shown standing beside his third wife, Jane Seymour, with his parents, Henry VII and Elizabeth of York, behind them. Of course, when Holbein was creating the mural, Henry VIII was the only one of these four still alive. Whitehall Palace burned down in 1698, and the painting was destroyed. Fortunately, it had been copied, though not particularly well, earlier in the century – this engraving of the mural derives from that copy.

Holbein's detailed preparatory drawing or 'cartoon' for the left-hand side of the mural has, however, survived. Henry's body, though visually striking, has some anatomical peculiarities, notably the deliberate flattery of elongating his legs (you can see this clearly if you compare the drawing with his armour in the Tower of London). The cartoon also strongly emphasises his masculinity. Holbein's powerful image of kingship was copied many times and has conditioned the way we perceive Henry VIII. It has been highly effective propaganda for the Tudors over the last 450 years.

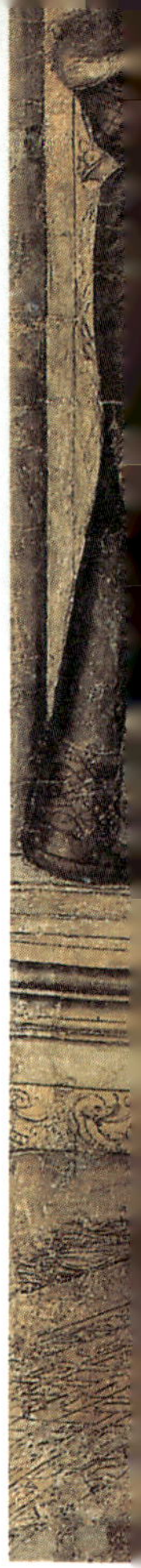

Elizabeth of York
Unknown artist, late 16th Century, after an original of c. 1500

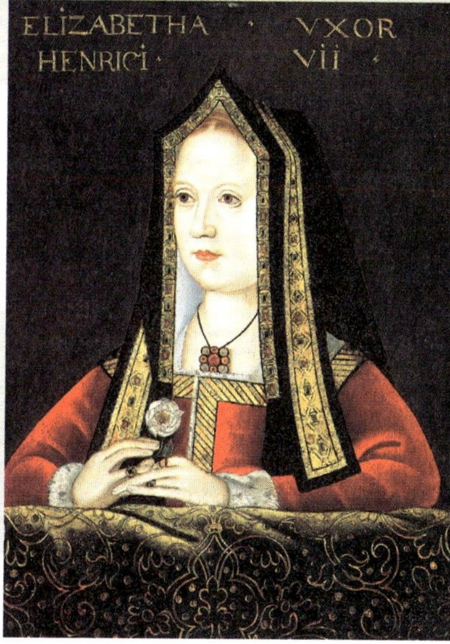

marriage did not in fact take place, but Margaret kept the portrait until her death.

Henry is shown as a European monarch, wearing the Order of the Golden Fleece awarded to him by Maxmilian I. The rose he holds symbolises both the Tudor dynasty and his role as a prospective lover. The composition also makes Henry appear to be looking through a window, with his hand on a sill. Towards the end of his life, Henry was described by his biographer as having 'small, blue eyes, a few poor black-stained teeth. His hair was thin and white: his complexion sallow'. Clearly his looks failed to win Margaret's heart.

Elizabeth of York (1465–1503), wife of Henry VII and mother of Henry VIII, was painted towards the end of her life. Unfortunately the original was lost and this is a copy, as are all surviving portraits of her. This picture was probably made as part of a set of kings and queens to hang in a country house.

The white rose she holds symbolises the House of York. It was Elizabeth's marriage to the Lancastrian Henry Tudor that brought to an end the Wars of the Roses, with the Tudor rose combining the red and white roses of the two warring factions. The painting is remarkably two-dimensional, making Elizabeth resemble the queen on a playing card. This effect is reinforced by the gable head-dress that both she and playing-card queens wear. The portrait is painted in a manner that emphasises ornament and decoration, for example her jewels and the gold threadwork on the cushions beneath her arms, rather than naturalistic representation. This difference in style is clearly highlighted by comparing the portrait with that of her husband, Henry VII (above left).

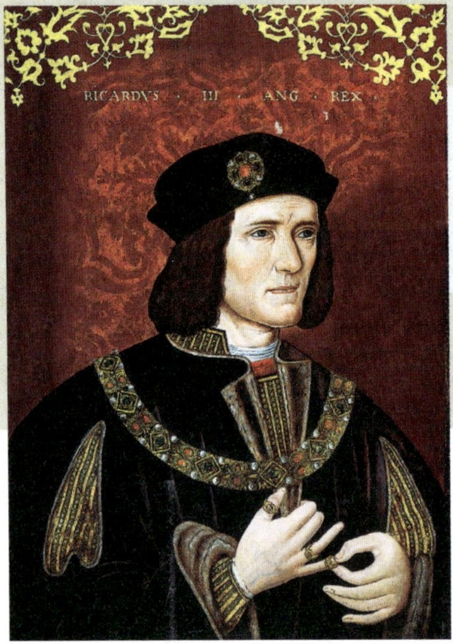

King Richard III
Unknown artist, late 16th Century, after an original of late 15th Century

Richard III (1452–85) was the last Yorkist king; his first biographer was Sir Thomas More, who wrote about him from a Tudor perspective. Richard loyally supported his brother Edward IV in his battles against the Lancastrians. However, after Edward's death, Richard sought the crown for himself during the minority of his nephew Edward V. When Edward V disappeared from the Tower of London with his younger brother in 1483, Richard achieved his ambition and was crowned King. The two boys are known to history as 'the princes in the Tower' and their precise fate remains a mystery to this day.

Richard met his death at the Battle of Bosworth Field, where he was defeated by the Lancastrian Henry Tudor. To put an end to the wars between the Houses of York and Lancaster, Henry married Richard's niece, Elizabeth of York. Richard III's reputation suffered denigration at the hands of the Tudors, including his portrayal by Shakespeare as an archetypal villain. A number of Richard's portraits also underwent later additions to emphasise a minor spinal problem, although there is little or no trace of it in this painting.

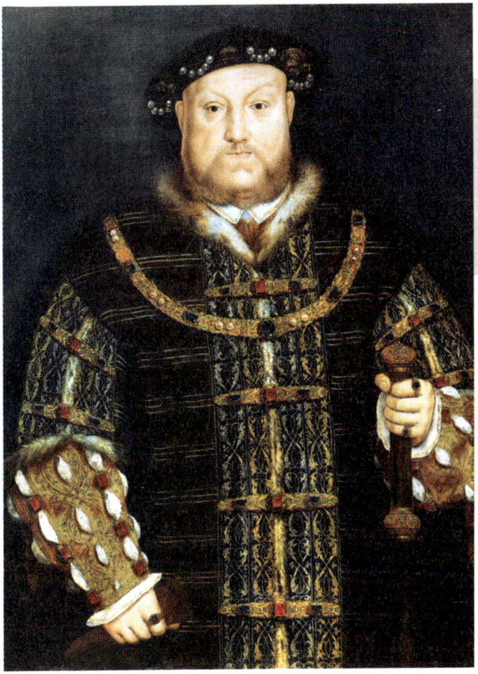

King Henry VIII
Unknown artist, perhaps early 17th Century, after an original of c. 1542

Although Holbein's original portrait of Henry VIII in old age did not survive, several copies exist and it has become a familiar image. It may well be that Henry did not sit to Holbein for this older portrait but that the artist merely 'aged' his earlier depictions of the king, also giving him the rich staff on which to support his large and by now ailing body. The original was probably painted a year or so before Holbein's own death in 1543.

Henry's face shows many of the features characteristic of Holbein's work. Interestingly, though contemporaries always commented on Holbein's incredible realism, he tended to paint slightly oddly proportioned faces, as is apparent here. The eyes are very wide apart and high in the face – more usual would be eyes half way down the head with about an eye's width between them. However, it is the sheer force and power of his images of Henry that have made these some of the best-known portraits from British history.

King Henry VIII;
King Henry VII;
Hans Holbein
the Younger,
c. 1536–37

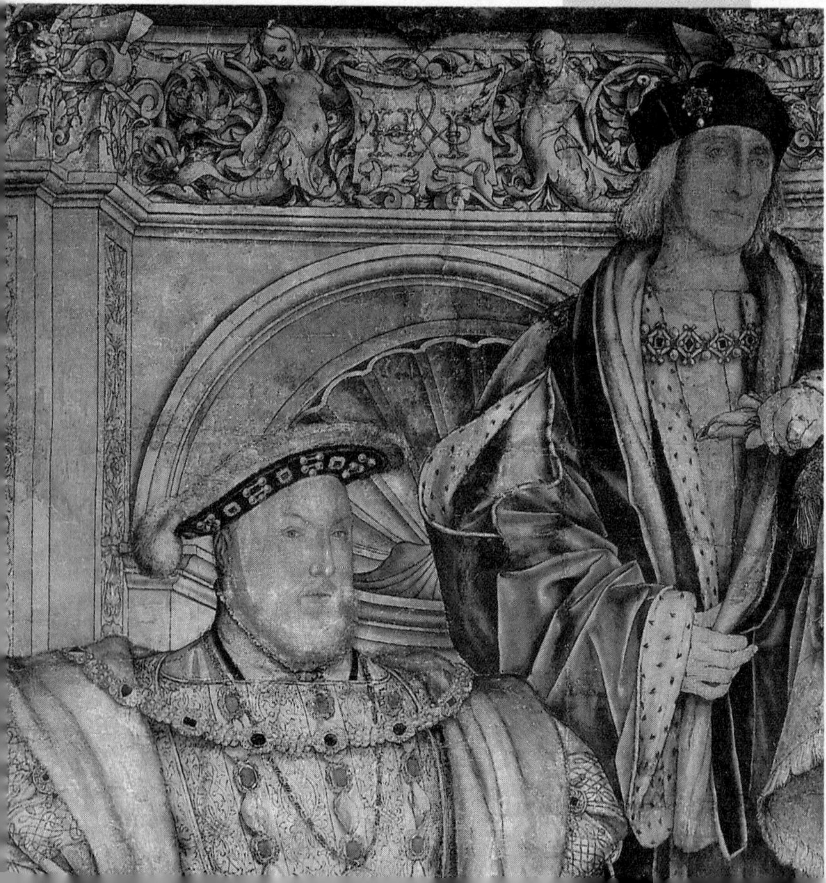

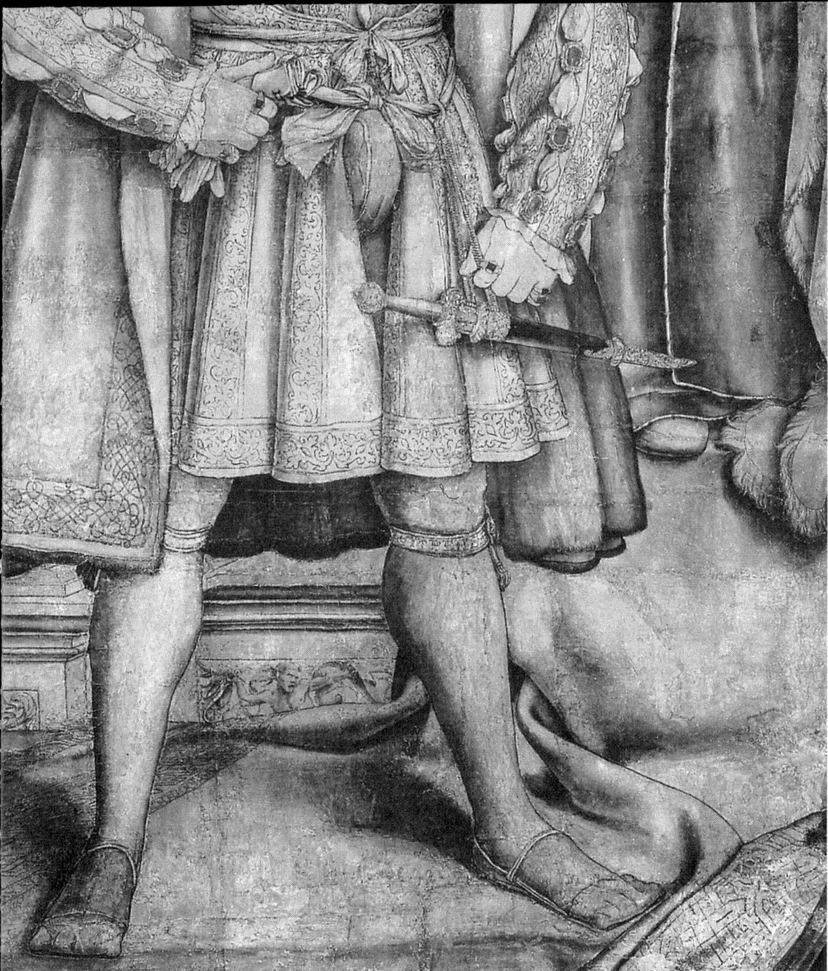

Holbein's intricate design was transferred to the wall to make the Whitehall Mural by a process known as 'pouncing'. The ink lines were pricked with tiny holes right through the paper. The pricked cartoon would be held up where the mural was to be and charcoal pushed through all the holes, making dots on the wall behind. Holbein then could join the dots and complete his mural in colour.

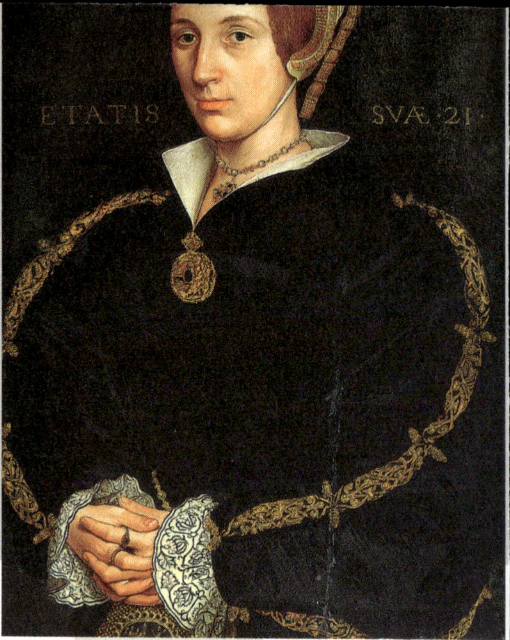

Unknown Woman, Formerly Known as Catherine Howard
Unknown artist, 16th Century, after Hans Holbein the Younger

Henry VIII's fifth wife (*died* 1542)

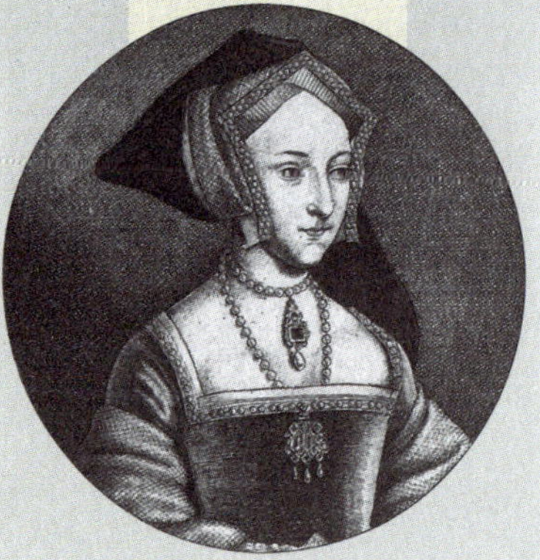

Jane Seymour
Wenceslaus Hollar, 1648, after Hans Holbein the Younger

Henry VIII's third wife (1509?–37)

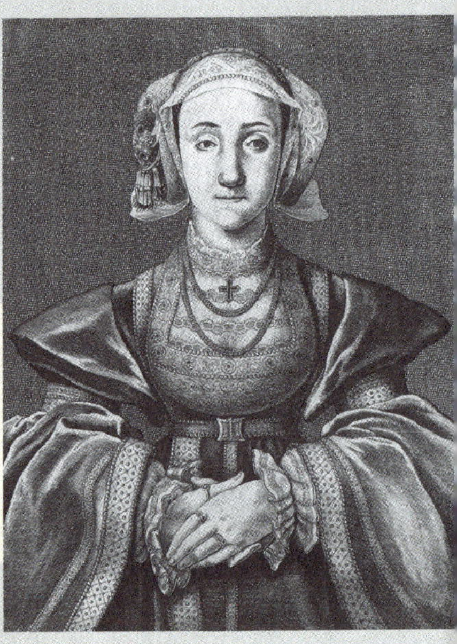

Anne of Cleves
Wenceslaus Hollar, 1648, after Hans Holbein the Younger

Henry VIII's fourth wife (1515–57)

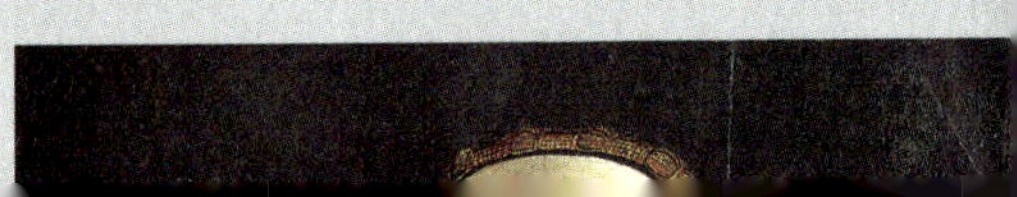

The Wives of King Henry VIII

The six women caught up in Henry VIII's matrimonial adventures became involved with the king in a variety of ways. Some, like Catherine of Aragon and Anne of Cleves, were pawns in supposedly advantageous foreign alliances. However, the swiftly shifting sands of European politics sometimes meant that by the time the bride reached the altar the alliance was already useless. Henry proposed various foreign marriages, most of which came to nothing. He employed artists such as Hans Holbein the Younger to paint his prospective wives; it is often said that Holbein's over-flattering portrait of Anne of Cleves played a part in Henry's disastrous fourth marriage, which rapidly ended in an annulment.

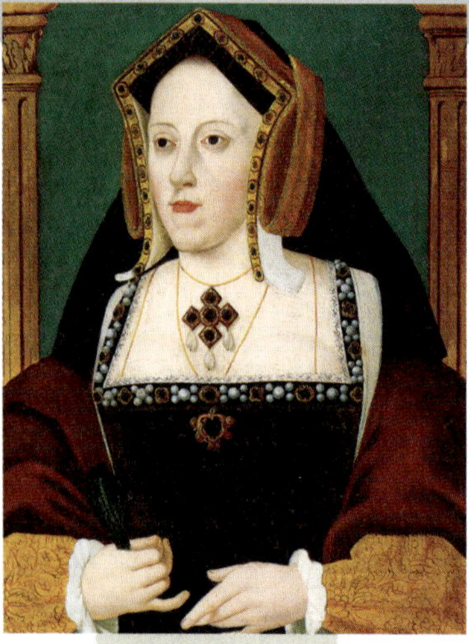

Catherine of Aragon
Unknown artist, after 1553

This portrait of Catherine of Aragon (1485–1536), Henry VIII's first wife, can be dated to the last decade of her life through the clothes she is wearing. By this time Catherine was beset by many troubles. Her only surviving child was a daughter, later to become Mary I, not the hoped-for son. Worse still, Henry VIII was trying to divorce Catherine so as to marry Anne Boleyn, as Catherine was beyond her child-bearing years. This divorce was to have momentous consequences, stretching far beyond Catherine herself. To achieve it, Henry broke away from the authority of the Pope and made himself head of the Church in England.

The Venetian Ambassador's secretary described Catherine as 'not of full stature, rather small. If not handsome she is not ugly; she is somewhat stout, and always has a smile on her countenance'. In her hand Catherine holds sprigs of greenery – symbolising, most ironically, fertility – while the shape of her jewelled pendant recalls her steadfast belief in the Roman Catholic faith.

Even more powerful in Henry's matrimonial motivation was his desire for a son. In different ways both Anne Boleyn and Jane Seymour paid for this with their lives, one through failure, the other through success. Henry was capable of genuinely falling in love but his jealousy led to the execution of two of his wives, Anne Boleyn and Catherine Howard, Henry's fifth wife (of whom there is no known likeness). Finally, Catherine Parr provided comfort in his old age, both for the king and for his three motherless children.

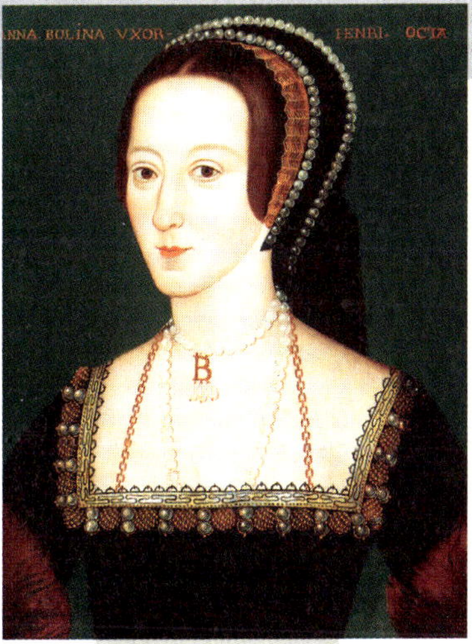

Anne Boleyn
Unknown artist,
late 16th Century,
after an original of
c. 1533–36

Comparing this portrait with that of Catherine of Aragon reveals, at least in part, Henry's motivation for divorcing the older woman and marrying as his second wife the vivacious Anne (1507–36). In her portrait Anne wears a jewelled letter 'B' for Boleyn.

Henry was so besotted with Anne that it was said she had bewitched him, but a Venetian diarist remarked that she was 'not one of the handsomest women in the world; she is of middling stature, swarthy complexion, long neck, wide mouth, bosom not much raised and in fact has nothing much but... her eyes which are black and beautiful.' Unfortunately for Anne, the king's passion decreased, especially after she gave birth to a daughter, later Elizabeth I, rather than to a male heir. She was accused of adultery and her 'long neck' was severed by the executioner's blade.

Catherine Parr
Attributed to
Master John,
c. 1545

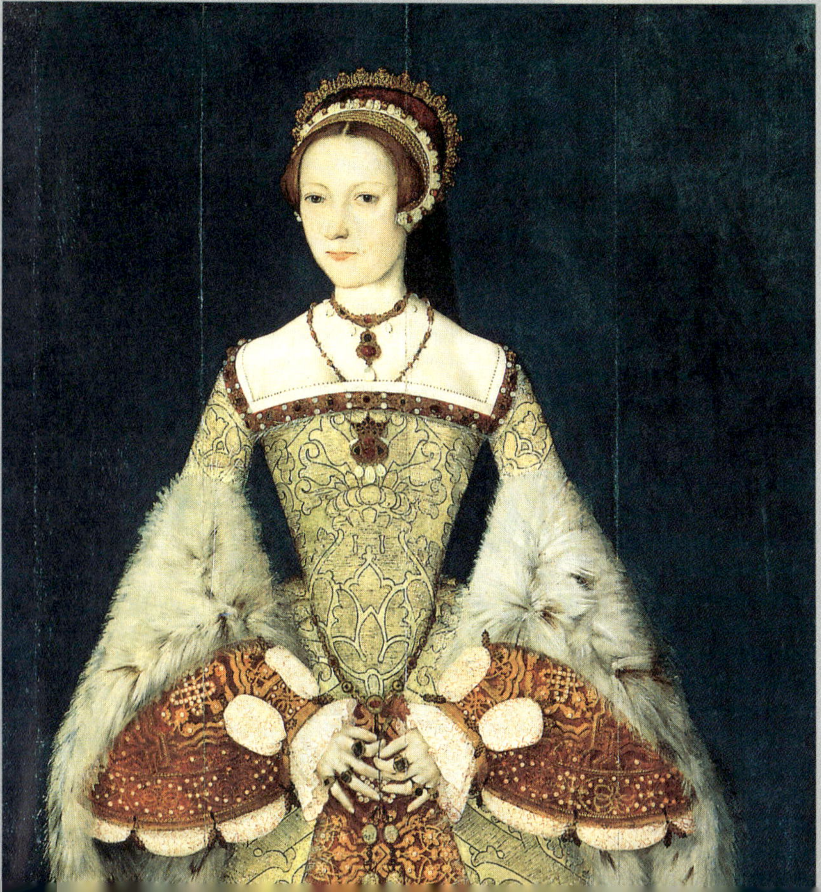

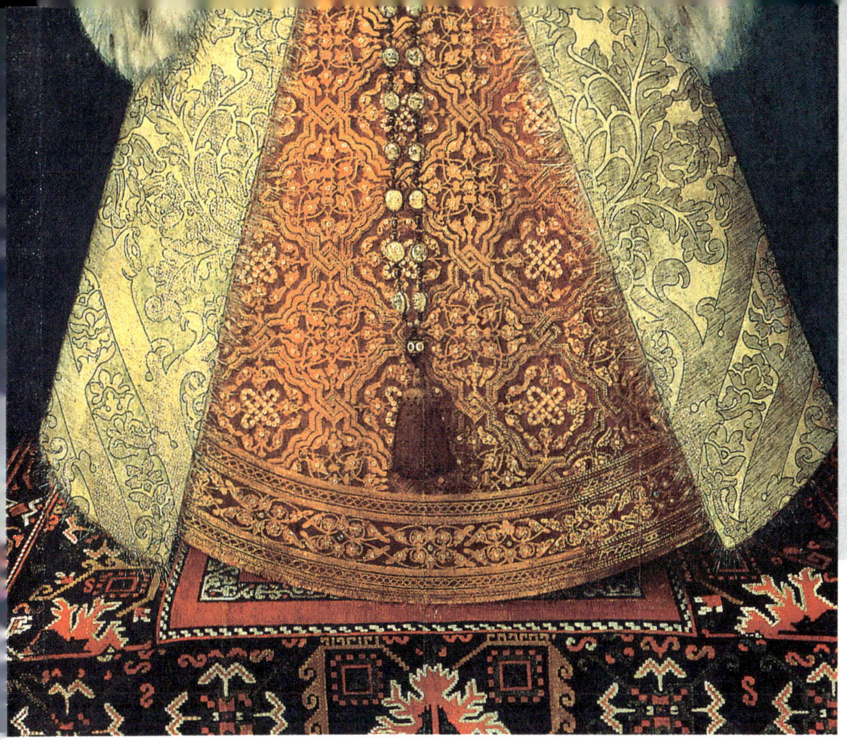

This portrait of Catherine Parr (1512–48) was painted during her three-and-a-half-year marriage to Henry VIII. Already twice widowed, Catherine had been on the verge of marrying Sir Thomas Seymour, one of the brothers of Henry's third queen, Jane Seymour. However, their union was 'overruled by a higher power' and instead she married the king as his sixth and last wife. On Henry's death, Thomas and Catherine were finally able to wed but Catherine herself died in childbirth just over a year later. A contemporary described her as combining 'a pregnant wittiness ... with right wonderful grace of eloquence'.

For many years the portrait was believed to be that of Lady Jane Grey (1537–54) around the age of eight. However, the older appearance of the sitter and the rarity of full-length portraits at that time raised doubts. The attribution to Henry's last queen was made when the distinctive brooch in this portrait – the three-pointed crown, four red gemstones and three pearls – was found described in an inventory of Catherine Parr's jewels.

Edward VI, the Boy King

Edward VI (1537–53) was Henry VIII's longed-for son and heir. He did not know his mother, Jane Seymour, as she died only twelve days after his birth. He came to the throne as a boy of nine, so the country was governed by a Council of Regency, first with Edward's uncle the Earl of Somerset as Lord Protector and then the Duke of Northumberland. Although the politics of his reign were largely dominated by the struggles between these two men, Edward was not without his own opinions, especially in matters of religion. He was a staunch Protestant and it was during his reign that the Book of Common Prayer was created, largely by Thomas Cranmer, Archbishop of Canterbury, which is still in occasional use today. In many ways Edward carried forward the reformation that had been initiated by his father when in search of a male heir.

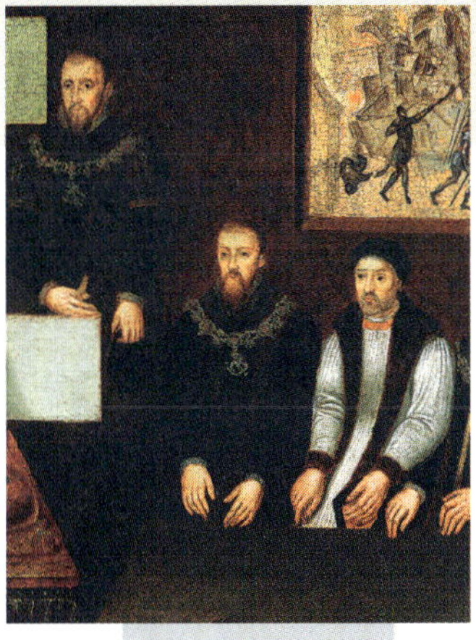

King Edward VI and the Pope
(detail of the Council of Regency)

In this detail from the painting *King Edward VI and the Pope*, it is not possible to identify with absolute certainty any of the members of the Council of Regency. However, three key figures stand out as strong possibilities. One is Edward Seymour, Earl of Somerset, the first Lord Protector, who is shown on his feet. Beside him may be his brother Thomas, who married the widowed Catherine Parr, though it has also been suggested that this is John Dudley, later Duke of Northumberland, the second Lord Protector. The next figure is almost certainly Thomas Cranmer, Archbishop of Canterbury.

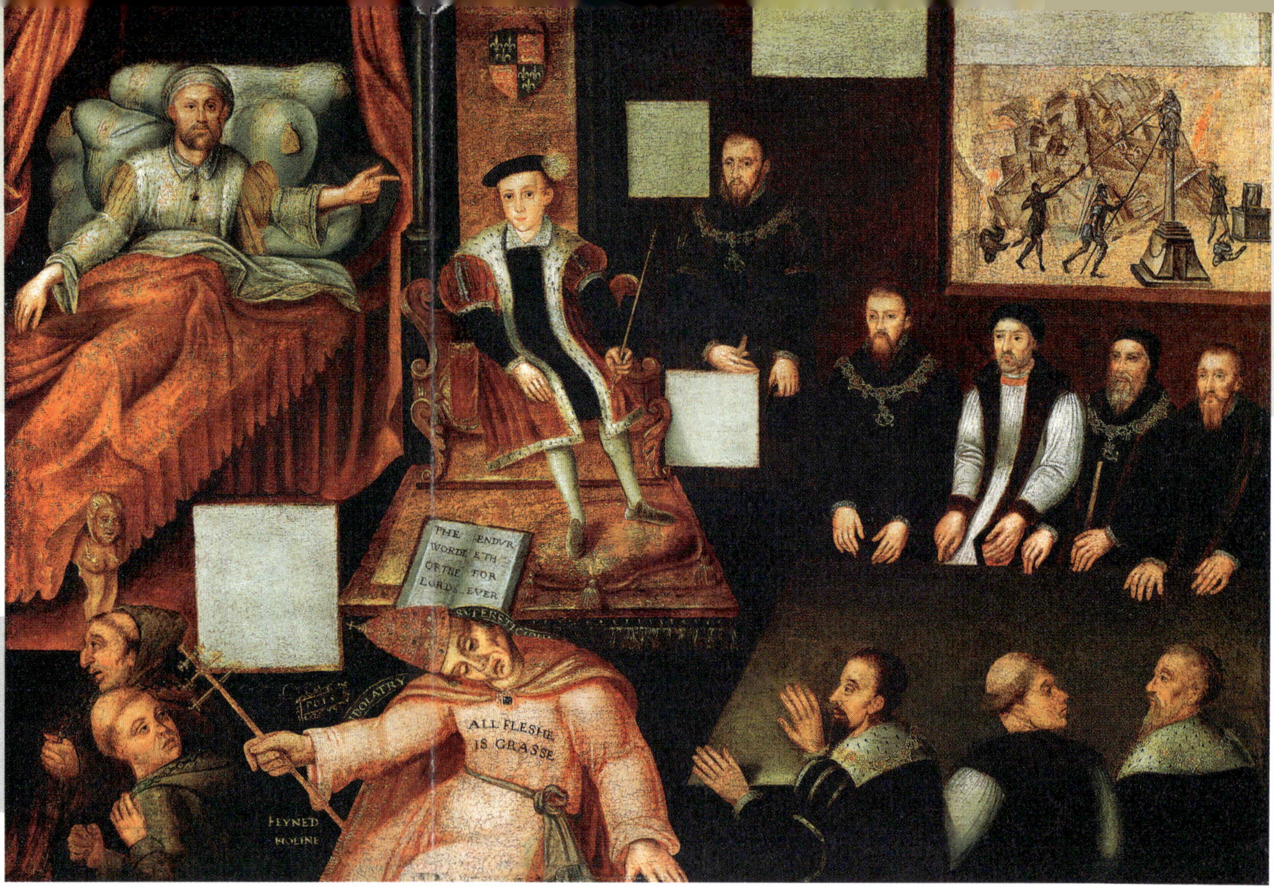

King Edward VI and the Pope
Unknown artist,
c. 1570

This portrait shows key events from the reign of the boy king, Edward VI, and depicts him sitting on the throne, holding a sceptre. To Edward's right lies Henry VIII on his deathbed, pointing to his son and heir. To Edward's left is the Council of Regency, which assisted him to rule during his minority. Below Edward is the Bible, translated into English, proclaiming 'the word of the Lord endureth for ever'. The Bible hits the Pope on the head, knocking him sideways – the words 'all flesh is grass' across his chest reinforce the message. The comatose Pope is being dragged away by two monks, inscribed 'feigned holiness', 'idolatory' and 'superstition'. In fact, the English Bible, the toppling of the Pope and the dissolution of the monasteries had already taken place under Henry VIII, before Edward came to the throne. In the top right-hand corner is a scene from Edward's own reign, showing the violent iconoclasm as Catholic images were declared idolatrous and smashed.

The painting itself has been the subject of recent reinterpretation. Research has shown that key visual elements, in particular the very distinctive carving at the foot of Henry's bed and the column in the iconoclasm scene, are copied from Dutch engravings of the later 1560s, therefore dating the picture to Elizabeth's reign, not to Edward's as was previously believed.

Mary I and the Mid-Century

Issues of religion dominated the middle years of the sixteenth century. Although King Henry VIII had broken away from the Church of Rome in the 1530s and Edward VI had made important doctrinal changes, it was several decades before England was irretrievably set on a Protestant course. With hindsight we can see the return to Catholicism under Mary I as a temporary reversal and the accession of Elizabeth to the throne as confirmation of Protestantism's lasting hold. However, it would not necessarily have seemed that way to people living through those years. English Protestantism was still a very new faith in need of nurturing, while the continuing insecurities fuelled lingering Catholic hopes of yet another reversal in their religious fortunes. Indeed, it encouraged some English Catholics to support the cause of the imprisoned Mary, Queen of Scots, while the threat from Catholic Spain under Philip II persisted with varying intensity throughout the later years of Elizabeth's reign.

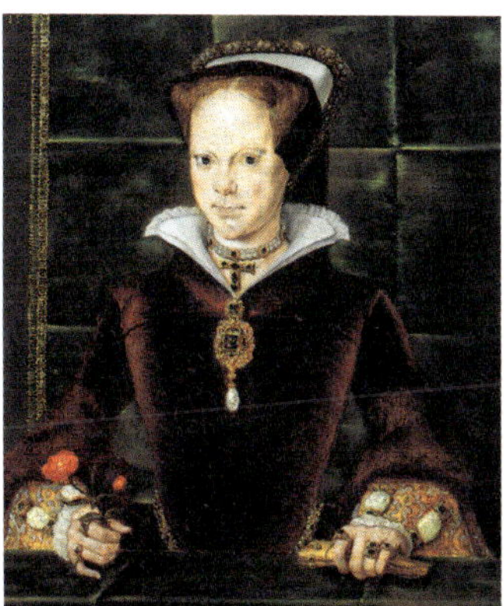

Queen Mary I
Hans Eworth, 1554

This portrait of Mary I (1516–58) was painted early in her reign, in 1554, around the time of her marriage to Philip II of Spain, which helped to bring England firmly back within the fold of Catholic Europe, albeit only for a short while. According to a Venetian visiting England that summer: 'She is low of stature, with a red and white complexion and very thin; her eyes are white and large, and her hair reddish; her face is round, with a nose rather low and wide; and were not her age on the decline she might be called handsome rather than the contrary.'

The large jewel on her dress seems almost certainly to have been a wedding present from Philip II. A Spanish contemporary described the gem as 'a great diamond with a large pearl pendant, one of the most beautiful pieces ever seen in the world'. In her right hand Mary holds a red rose, a symbol of love and beauty as well as the emblem of the Tudors, while her left hand, holding her gloves, displays a fine array of rings.

Thomas Cranmer
Gerlach Flicke, 1545

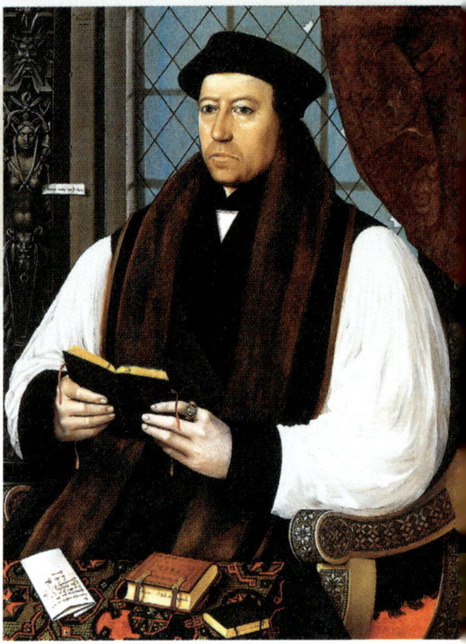

This portrait was painted during Henry VIII's reign and shows the Archbishop of Canterbury, Thomas Cranmer (1489–1556), reading St Paul's *Epistles*. As Henry's archbishop, Cranmer played a vital role in steering through the king's divorce from Catherine of Aragon, his subsequent marriage to Anne Boleyn and the passing of the Act of Supremacy making Henry, not the Pope, head of the Church in England. During Edward's reign the programme of reform continued with the introduction of the Book of Common Prayer, Cranmer's great contribution to English literature as well as worship.

Cranmer's Protestantism led him reluctantly to support Lady Jane Grey in the abortive plot to exclude the Catholic Mary Tudor from the throne. Retribution was swift to follow. Mary stripped him of his archbishopric and had him imprisoned. He made a partial reconversion to Roman Catholicism before being burnt at the stake in Oxford. However, as the flames rose, he recanted, thrusting into the fire his right hand with which he had signed his Catholic confession, and died reaffirming his Protestant faith

Queen Elizabeth I, The Coronation Portrait
Unknown artist, c.1600, after an original of c.1559?

This painting is a posthumous copy – the original Coronation Portrait has not survived – but it is nonetheless a majestic image. Elizabeth I (1533–1603) is depicted wearing her crown, and holding the orb and sceptre. Her robes, which were woven with gold and silver thread and lined with ermine, are decorated with Tudor roses and fleurs-de-lis, symbolising the English claim to French soil. Significantly, these robes were not made specifically for Elizabeth's coronation in 1559; they had been worn five years earlier by her sister Mary I for her own coronation, when England still was in possession of Calais.

As well as the crown jewels and golden robes, aspects of Elizabeth's appearance mark this out as a Coronation Portrait. She is, for example, shown full-face, an unusual arrangement in Tudor portraiture but one that was repeated on her coinage. Queens were traditionally crowned with their hair loose and flowing in this manner.

Elizabeth's hairline, which would have been achieved through plucking, is unnaturally high to give the desired face shape of the Tudors, long and thin. On her temples blue 'veins' have been painted over the white make-up to give the impression of gossamer-thin skin.

King Edward VI, Anamorphosis
(two views)
William Scrots,
1546

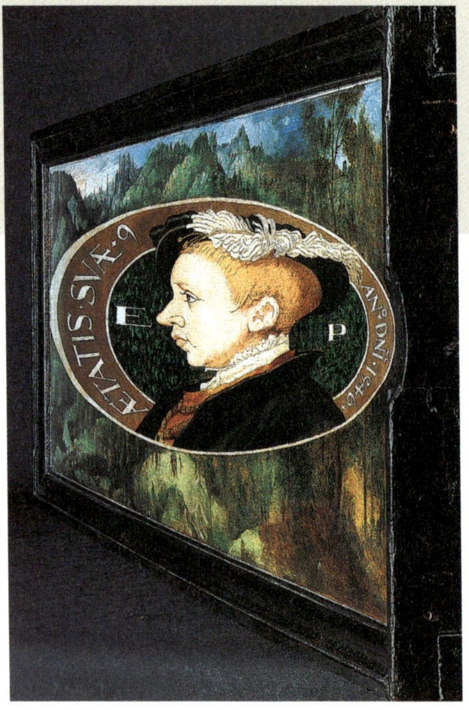

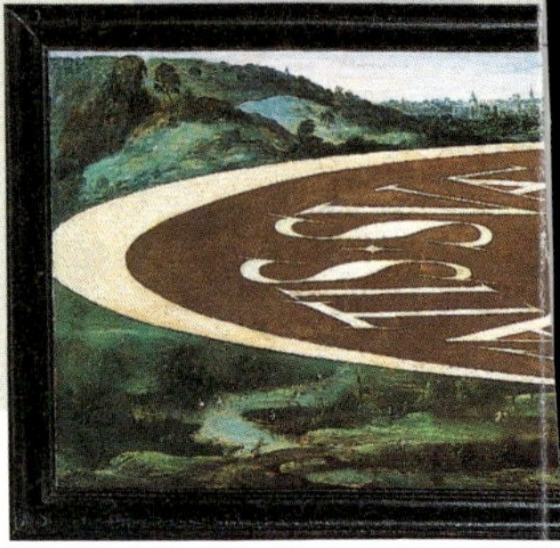

The whiteness of Edward's skin is deliberate; children of both sexes, as well as women, had white lead-based make-up applied to their faces during the second half of the sixteenth century. Although to us the white skin might suggest ill-health, to the Tudors it was a sign of beauty.

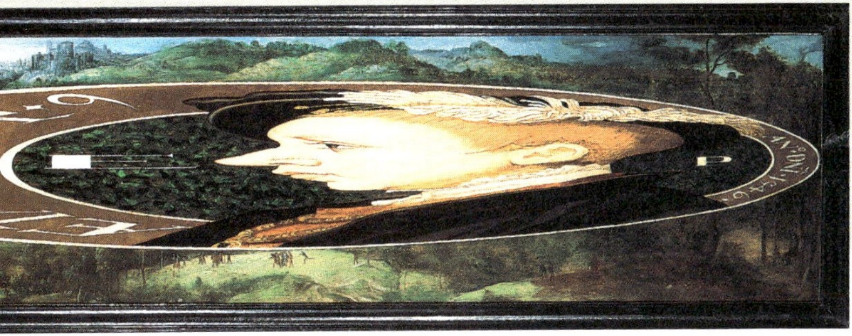

This unusual portrait of Edward VI was painted when he was aged nine, probably in the year he became king. It may have been created to entertain him, rather as children today enjoy optical illusions. It also served to show off the painter's talents as this type of 'stretched' image, called an anamorphosis, was quite a novelty in England, though not unknown, having been used by Holbein to conceal a skull in his great portrait of *The Ambassadors*, now in the National Gallery. When viewed from a certain point to the right of the painting, Edward appears in correct perspective.

The landscape in the corners was added later, probably around 1600. We know that this portrait was an object of great wonder when it was in the Royal Collection, though it was sold off very cheaply after the execution of Charles I in the mid-seventeenth century, when such visual tricks were no longer so highly prized.

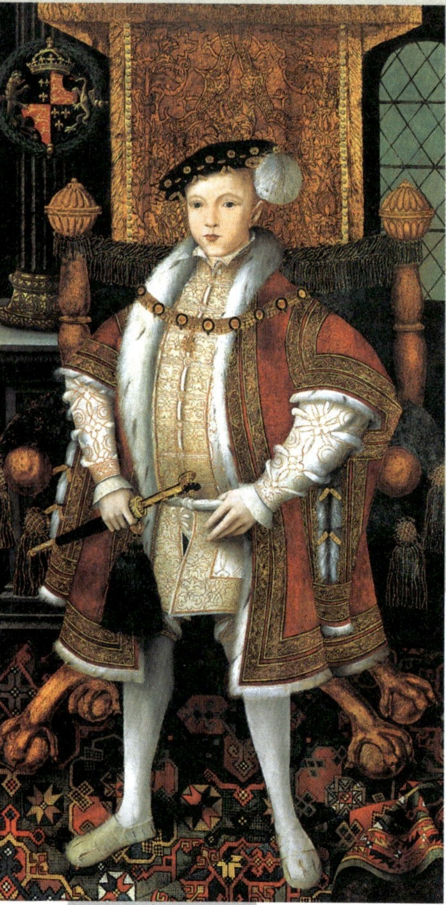

King Edward VI
Unknown artist,
c. 1547

This portrait of Edward VI was painted around the time of his father's death and his own accession to the throne at the age of nine. Edward stands in the pose devised by Holbein for Henry VIII in the Whitehall Mural. The portrait is meant to invest the boy with his father's strength, masculinity and power – the legs firmly apart, the hand grasping the dagger and the placing of the figure in the centre foreground all work towards this interpretation. However, the total effect fails to convince. Edward's thin legs, and the fact that his rich clothes have so obviously been stuffed to give him his father's manly shape, detract from the impression of strength.

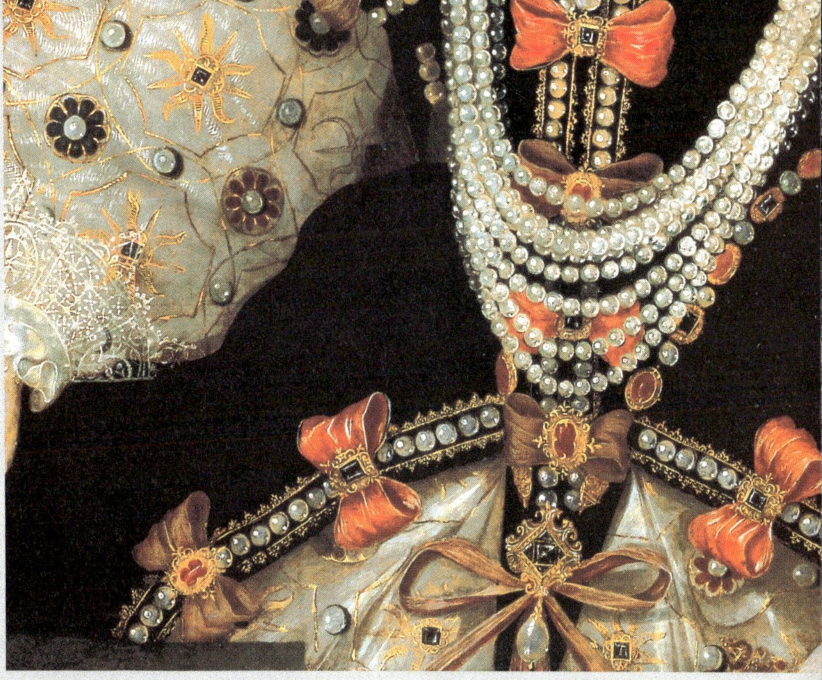

When this painting was first acquired by the National Portrait Gallery, Elizabeth appeared to be standing in front of green curtains, with no ships visible. However, the curtains were found to be a later addition and cleaning revealed the Armada scenes underneath.

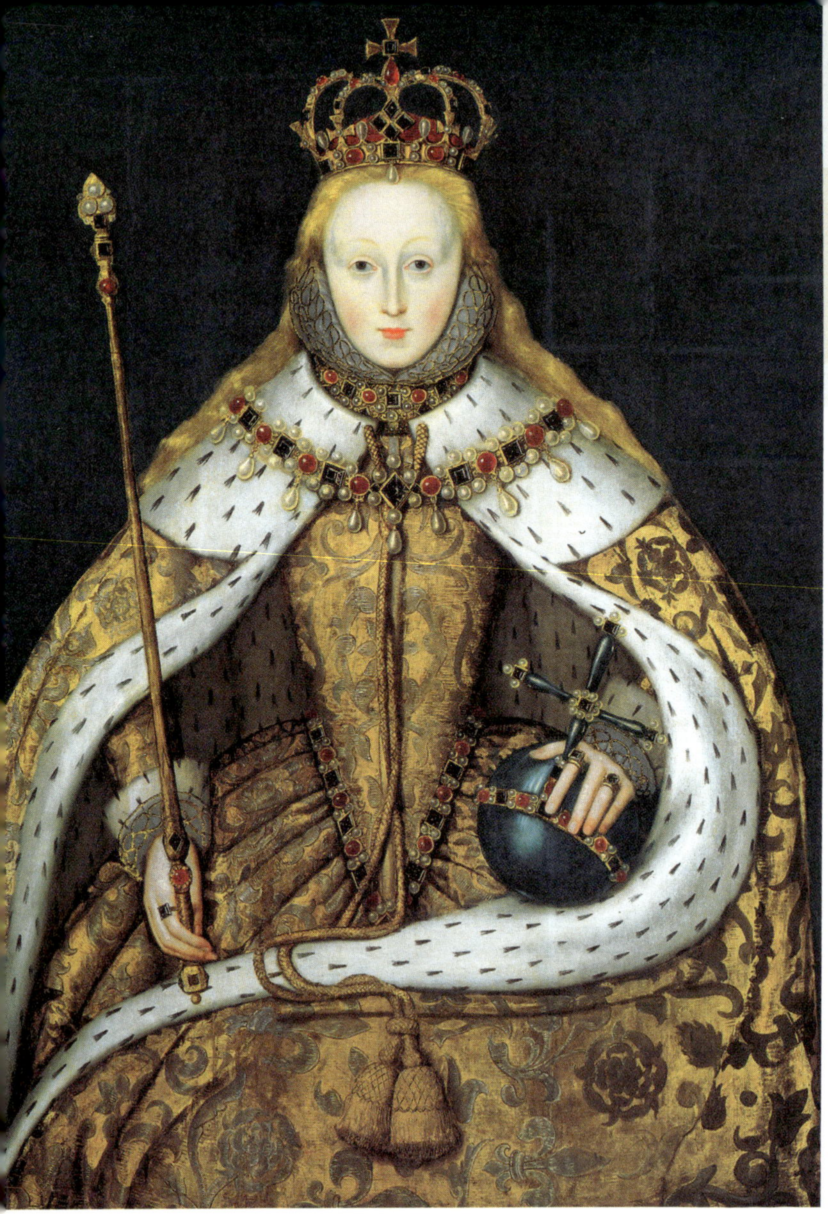

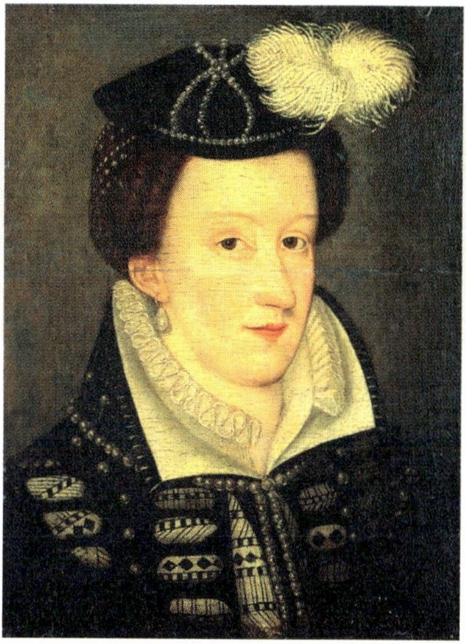

Mary, Queen of Scots
Unknown artist,
after a miniature of
c. 1560–65

Mary Stuart (1542–87), Elizabeth I's Roman Catholic cousin, became Queen of Scotland when she was just a few days old. Although Mary and Elizabeth were bitter adversaries, culminating in Mary's execution, it was her son James who was made King of England when Elizabeth I died without leaving an heir. Mary's life, however, is remembered mainly for her various marriages and for her own claims to the throne of England, which led her into conflict with her royal cousin.

Mary's first marriage was to the King of France, in the year of Elizabeth's accession. She was widowed at 18 and returned to Scotland, where she married Lord Darnley, a descendant of Henry VII and a possible heir to the throne of England. Mary was known for her beauty; this portrait shows her during these years in Scotland, around the time of her marriage to Darnley, after which her life began severely to unravel. Following the death of Darnley in 1567 Mary married again, this time to her late husband's murderer. Mary's reputation was irrevocably damaged and in the following year, as opposition to her rule increased in Scotland, she fled to England for refuge. Unfortunately for Mary, she was taken prisoner by Queen Elizabeth and was to remain a captive for the next 19 years, ever a focus for Catholic plots and therefore a continuing threat to Elizabeth. She was executed at Fotheringay early in 1587.

This portrait was painted around 1580, so it was a more youthful-looking Philip II of Spain (1527–1598) who married Mary I in 1554. Highly unpopular as a Roman Catholic and a foreigner, he spent little time in England, especially when Mary failed to produce the much anticipated heir. By the time this portrait was painted, Mary was dead, and relations between England and Spain had deteriorated. It was Philip who, in 1588, ordered the Armada to sail against the kingdom of Elizabeth I.

The portrait shows Philip in ornate ceremonial armour with a mass of ostrich plumes rising from his helmet; in his hand he holds a commander's baton. Armour followed the fashions in clothing at the time, and copied men's jackets which were cut with the same projecting 'peascod' shape as Philip's breast-plate. Around his neck Philip wears the continental Order of the Golden Fleece and the painter has made a fine display of Philip's legs, again following contemporary fashion.

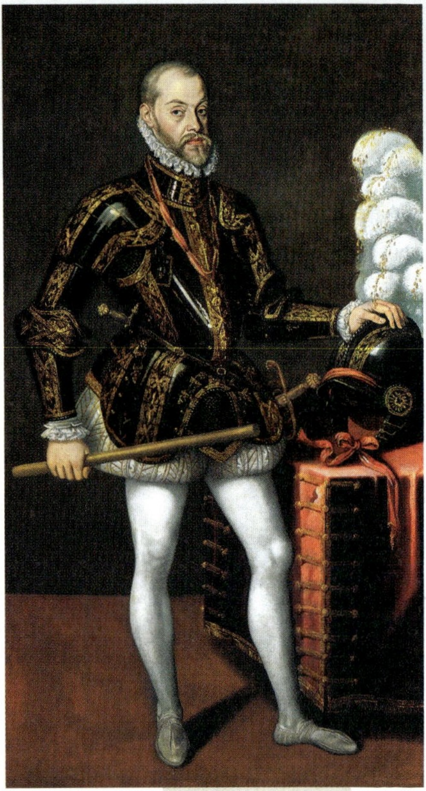

Philip II, King of Spain
Unknown artist, c. 1580

Queen Elizabeth I, The Armada Portrait
Attributed to George Gower, c. 1588

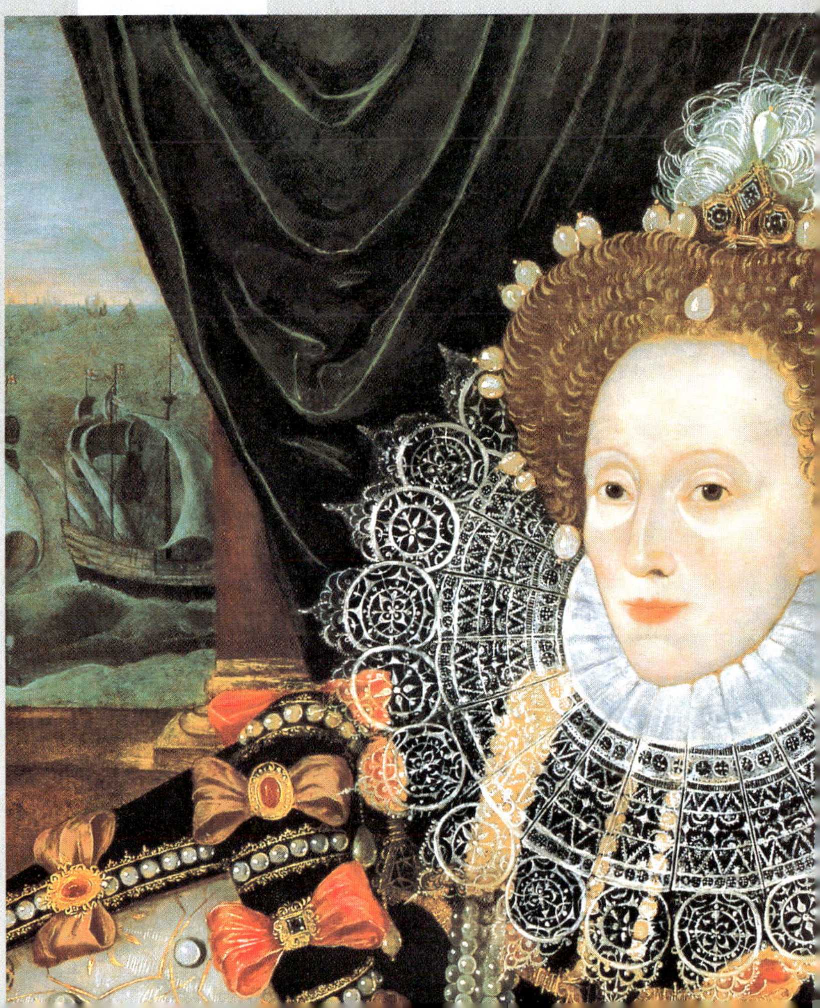

Elizabeth and the Spanish Armada

The defeat of the Spanish Armada was one of the high points of Elizabeth's reign and remains one of the best-remembered events in Tudor history. However, the Armada battle was not fought in isolation but as part of a much longer campaign waged by Elizabeth in support of the Protestants in the Netherlands. She went to their aid in 1585 when they rebelled against religious oppression in the Spanish Empire under the staunchly Catholic King Philip II. Much of the fighting was on land in the Low Countries. This took place under the leadership of the Earl of Leicester although some of the more spectacular moments of the war were naval engagements associated with Sir Francis Drake. As well as the routing of the Armada, Drake's achievements included the burning of the Spanish fleet in Cadiz harbour, described as him 'singeing the King of Spain's beard'.

Both Drake and Leicester sat to the great miniature painter Nicholas Hilliard, as did Elizabeth herself. Hilliard wrote a manual which contains fascinating details of the process of miniature painting. The skin colour, called carnation, was applied first. The small black dots in pearls, such as those on Drake's buttons, were originally silver, burnished with a squirrel's tooth, but have since tarnished. Hilliard also provides useful practical advice if your paint should fail to adhere to your miniature: pick your ear and add the wax to your paint.

Sir Francis Drake
Nicholas Hilliard,
1581

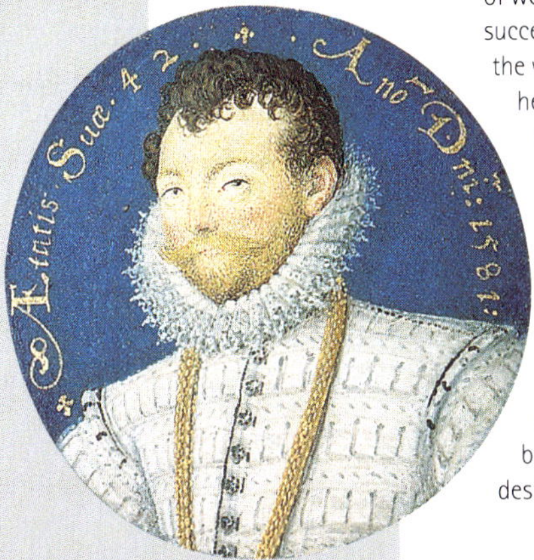

Unusually for the time, Sir Francis Drake (1540?–96) was born into poverty but died a rich man. This portrait miniature shows him already well established with fine clothes and other trappings of wealth. It is dated 1581, the year after Drake successfully completed his circumnavigation of the world, the first Englishman so to do. In 1581 he was knighted by Queen Elizabeth on his ship the *Golden Hinde*, one of the highlights of his career.

Drake took centre stage again when in 1588 the English Navy defeated the much larger Spanish force. Even though Drake was not the commander in charge, his brilliant tactic of attacking the Spanish fleet with fire ships was a dramatic success, particularly as it was followed by a spectacular storm, which sealed the destruction of the fleeing Armada.

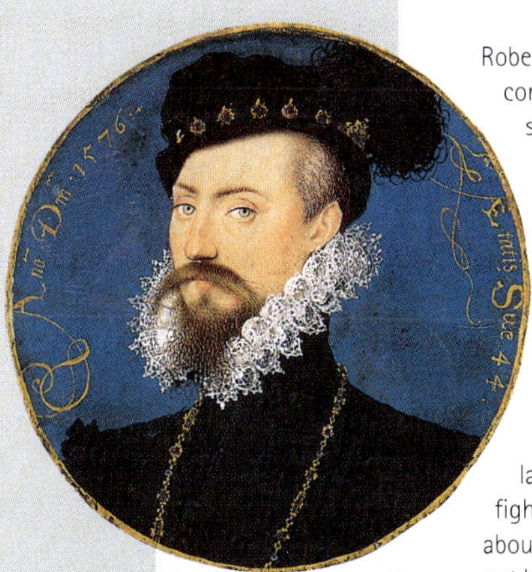

Robert Dudley, Earl of Leicester
Nicholas Hilliard,
1576

Robert Dudley (1532?–88) was described by a contemporary as 'a very goodly person, and singular well-featured, and all his youth well favoured and of a sweet aspect but... he grew high coloured and red-faced.' Certainly, he impressed Elizabeth I; he was a long-standing favourite and the one that she came nearest to marrying, despite the fact that he was already married by the time of her accession to the throne.

Leicester was made both a Privy Councillor and a Knight of the Garter and later became commander of the English troops fighting the Spanish in the Netherlands. Rumours about his relationship with the queen abounded, not least when his wife, Amy Robsart, was found dead, possibly murdered. It was even said that her death was part of a plot to free Leicester so that he could marry Elizabeth. However, such rumours actually rendered their marriage an impossibility.

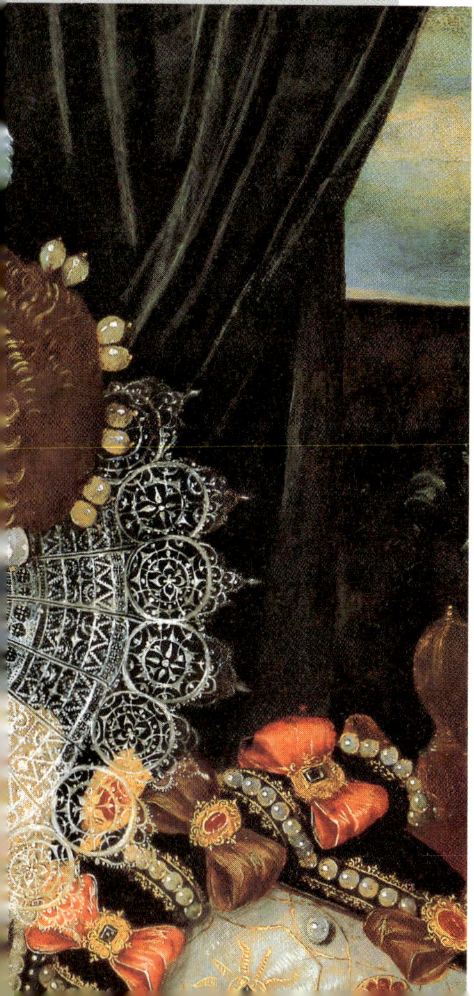

This magnificent portrait of Elizabeth I bedecked in jewels and gold-embroidered robes celebrates one of the most prestigious periods of her reign: the victory of her navy over the Spanish Armada. It can be dated to 1588, the year of the battle, or shortly after.

Now much reduced from its original size, perhaps to save the central section from an attack of woodworm, the painting would once have shown rather more than the figure of Elizabeth resplendent in her striking dress. Two surviving copies help to reveal the missing details. Behind the queen are two dramatic scenes, one of the English fleet unleashing its fire ships at the start of the battle and the other of the wreck of the Spanish ships in the storm. These two different moments in the conflict are pictured as if happening simultaneously, just over Elizabeth's shoulder. The original portrait would have also included her crown and a globe, reinforcing her majesty and her claim to rule not just a country but an empire.

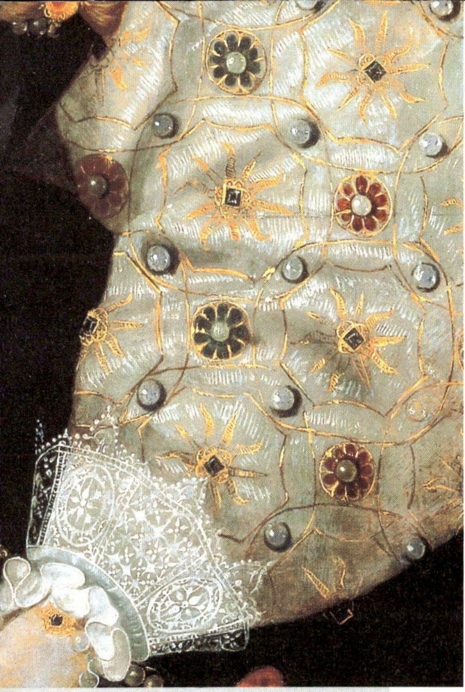

This painting seems to have been made for Elizabeth's first visit to Sir Henry Lee's house after a two-year absence while he was out of favour. The references to their quarrel and later reconciliation are clear, with the storms and sunshine as a metaphor for Elizabeth's decision to put her anger behind her and forgive him for his errant ways. Commissioned by Lee to paint Elizabeth, Marcus Gheeraerts the Younger balanced flattery with realism in producing this image of the ageing queen. Familiar themes are restated, with the spectacular white dress reflecting her virginity, and the rose pinned to her ruff symbolising both beauty and the House of Tudor.

The Ditchley Portrait offers some important political messages. Elizabeth is standing with her feet on a map of England, proclaiming her domination over her kingdom; the presence of the globe beneath her suggests an aspiration to imperial power. The background with its storms and sunshine further reinforces her glory and status, celebrating her having successfully brought the country through tumultuous times to its present happy state. The storms of the portrait also recall the unforgettable destruction of the Spanish Armada, as do the English ships around the coastline.

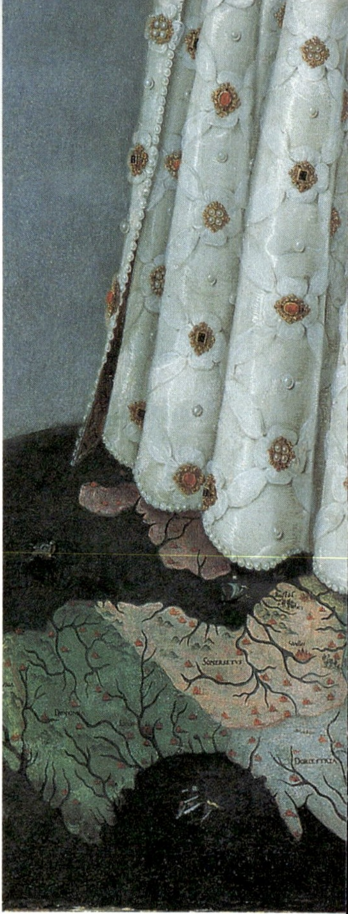

Queen Elizabeth I, The Ditchley Portrait
Marcus Gheeraerts the Younger, c. 1592

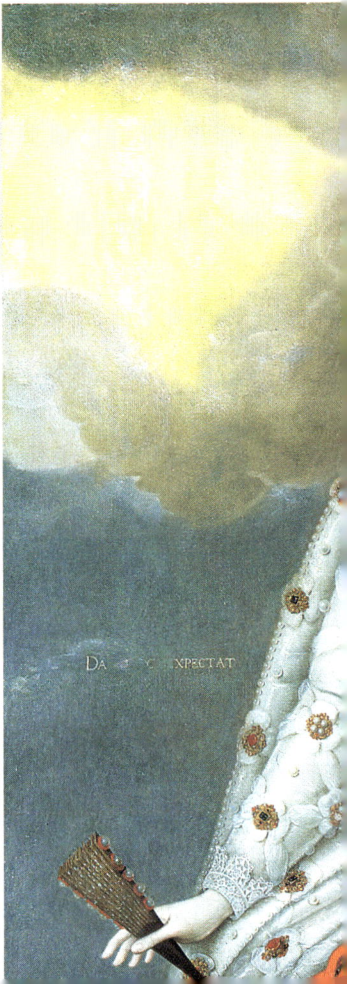

Elizabeth, the Later Years

As a result of her refusing to commit herself to one man and marry, the image of Elizabeth I as the Virgin Queen was a familiar one and was even alluded to by Shakespeare in *A Midsummer Night's Dream*. Elizabeth herself employed it to manage her courtiers, such as Sir Henry Lee; she triumphantly proclaimed her chastity and welcomed the attention inherent in being the unattainable lady of courtly love. Her courtiers in turn spoiled her with shows of affection, employing portraiture as well as poetry in their endeavours to win the heart of their honoured queen.

In her later portraits, by which time it was clear that Elizabeth would not marry, the English queen's virginity received a strong visual emphasis. She appeared frequently in paintings in her favourite colours of black and white, adorned with a mass of pearls. Pearls were symbolic because of their resemblance to the full moon. The moon was associated with chastity, since in classical mythology the moon goddess, who was variously called Diana or Cynthia, was a virgin.

William Shakespeare (1564–1616) is celebrated, the world over, as the greatest English playwright of his or, indeed, any age. He has been studied for hundreds of years but remains a somewhat enigmatic figure. His portraiture also raises problems, there being no indisputable likeness surviving from Shakespeare's lifetime. This portrait, however, can safely be said to have a greater claim to authenticity than any other painting, both because of its age and its similarities to the famous engraving from the printed editions of Shakespeare's plays and the monument to him in Stratford-upon-Avon Church.

Elizabeth as the Virgin Queen appears in *A Midsummer Night's Dream*, during a speech by Oberon in which he explains to Puck how the juice of the flower 'love-in-idleness' came to have the power to make people fall in love with the first thing they see. Shakespeare describes Elizabeth I as 'a fair vestal thronèd by the west' at whom Cupid aimed his 'fiery shaft', which missed her and fell instead on the flower:

'And the imperial votaress
passed on
In maiden meditation, fancy-
free.'
(Act II, Scene 1)

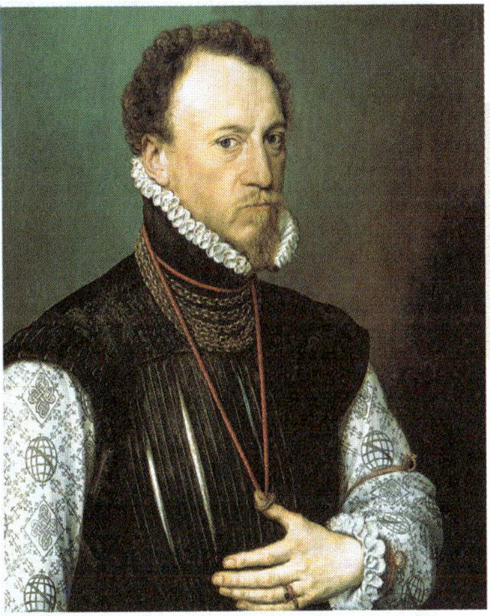

Sir Henry Lee
Antonis Mor, 1568

This portrait was painted in Antwerp in 1568, while Sir Henry Lee (1533–1611) was travelling around Europe. The peculiar detail of Lee's thumb hanging in a ring from a cord round his neck occurs in other portraits by Antonis Mor, but its significance remains unclear. Lee was, for most of her reign, Queen Elizabeth I's personal champion.

Sir Henry Lee was responsible for commissioning the full-length Ditchley Portrait of Elizabeth I, which epitomises her as the Virgin Queen. Lee had for a while fallen out of favour with Elizabeth when he had taken a mistress; the portrait appears to have played a role in the elaborate ceremonies that he orchestrated for a visit of reconciliation. The queen is pictured in a white dress, symbolic of purity. The portrait also includes various allusions to her relationship with Lee. Elizabeth is shown standing on a map with her feet on his estate at Ditchley in Oxfordshire. The celestial spheres that decorate Lee's sleeves in his own portrait by Mor form part of the symbolism by which he expressed his loyalty to her; the queen is shown wearing below her ear a celestial sphere similar to that on Lee's sleeves.

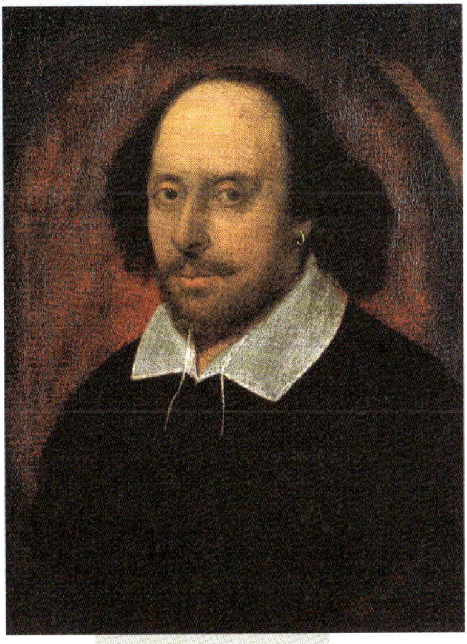

William Shakespeare
Attributed to
John Taylor, c. 1610

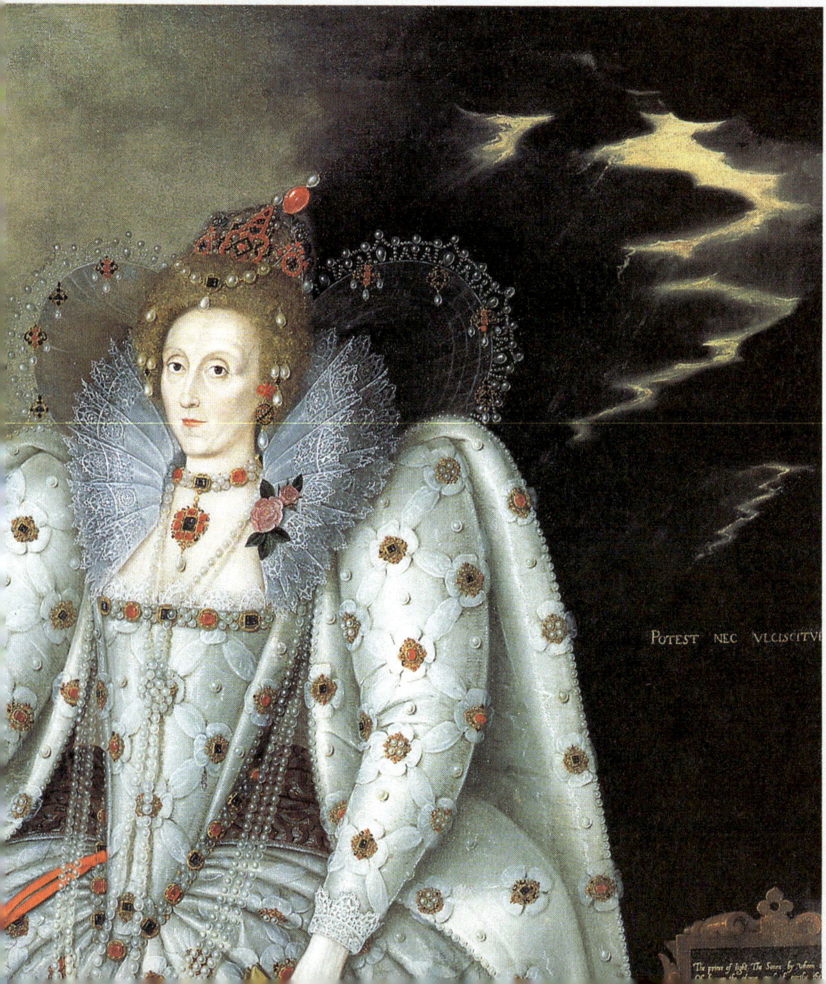
POTEST NEC VLCISCITV

The Life and Death of Sir Henry Unton

Tudor history was not just created by the very famous. Less celebrated people helped shape, and were themselves shaped by the events of the sixteenth century. One such man was the Elizabethan ambassador Sir Henry Unton, far less known to posterity than Drake or Leicester but nonetheless possessor of a fascinating life story, which, in a unique survival from Tudor times, is shown in the biographical painting that serves as a memorial to him.

Unlike Thomas More, with whom this book began, Henry Unton and his wife had no children to perpetuate their family line. Indeed it may have been this very fact that led Dorothy Unton, when widowed in 1596, to take the unusual step of commissioning a portrait to record not only her husband's appearance but the whole story of his life. This picture reveals to us not just fascinating details about his worldly surroundings but also his aspirations. Additionally, it allows us to witness the highpoint of his career, which was, bizarrely, his magnificent burial, following his death in France at the age of barely forty. Beside Henry himself, the key figure in this story is his mother Lady Anne Seymour, Countess of Warwick, as it was his desire to rise to the status she had once enjoyed that motivated Henry throughout his life and which, ironically, he came nearest to achieving at his funeral.

Sir Henry Unton
(Detail)

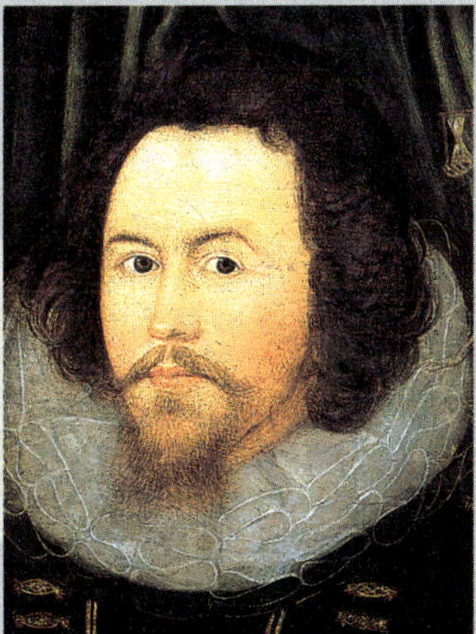

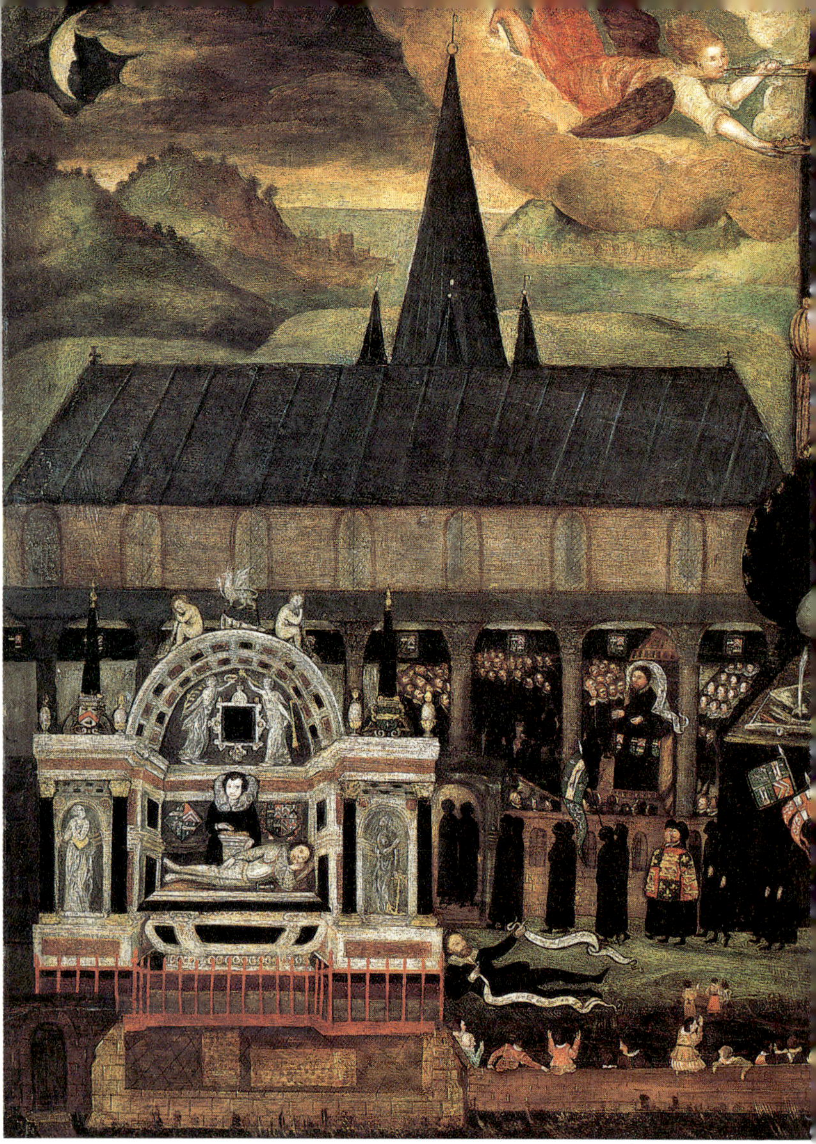

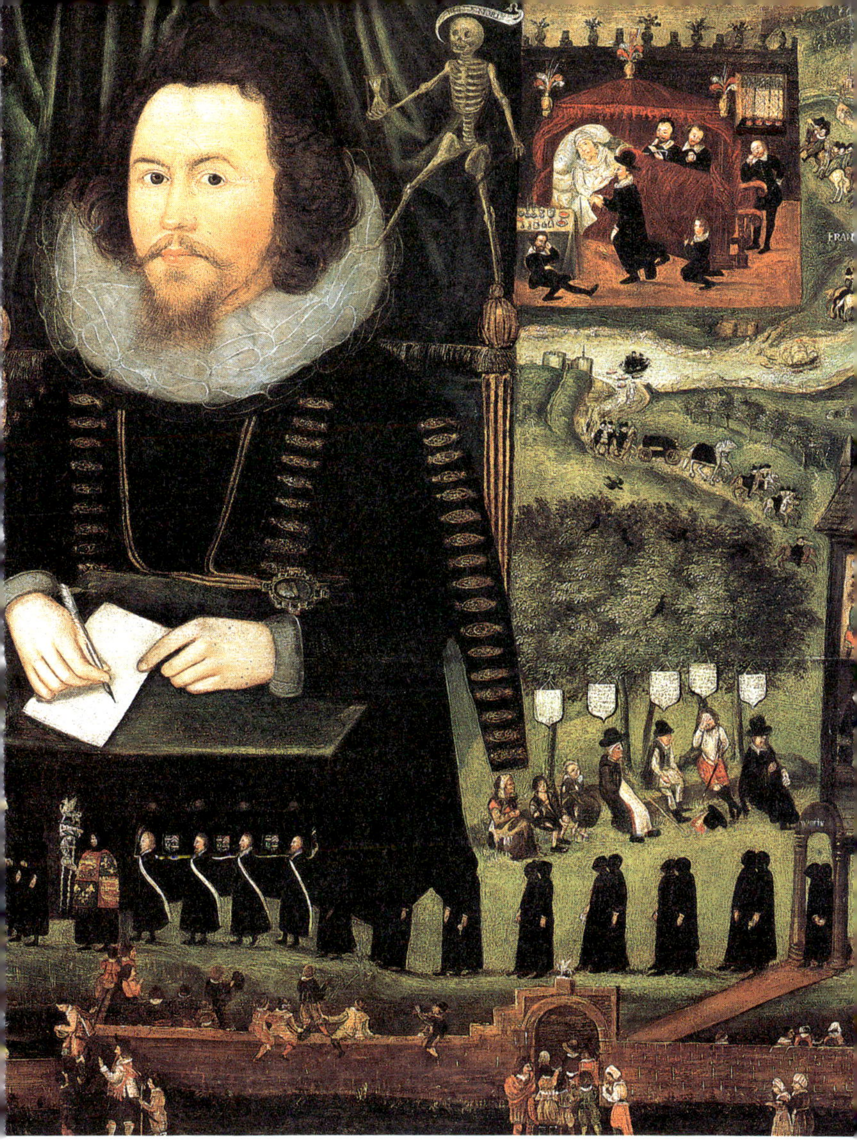

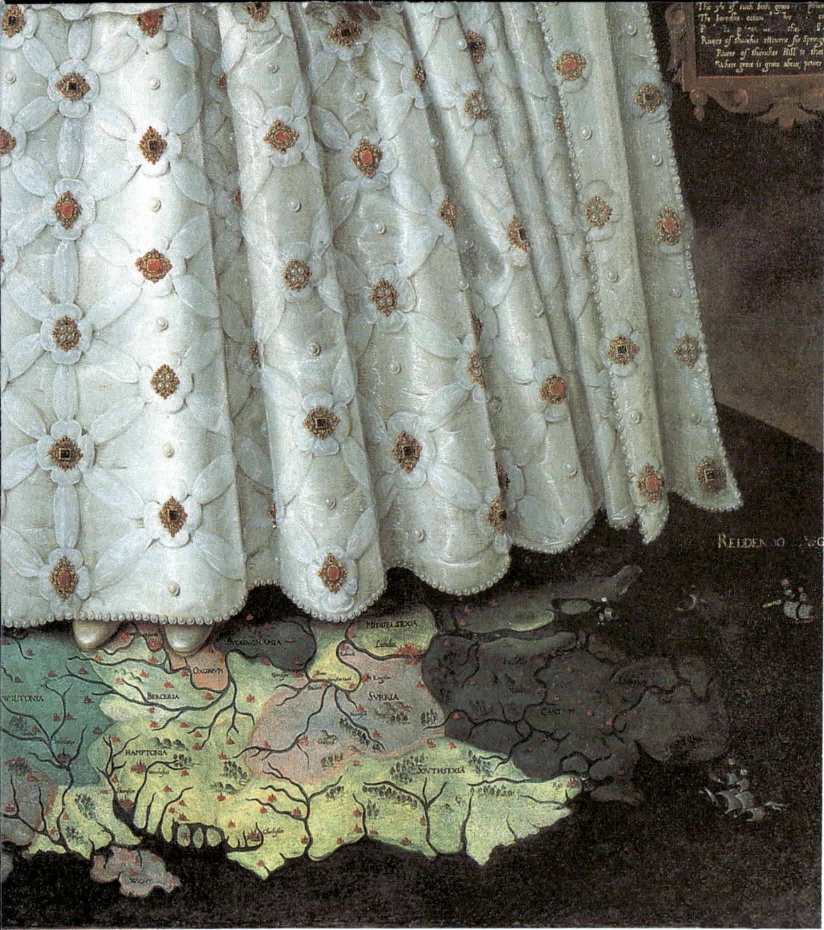

This portrait of Elizabeth when originally painted was about 20 cm wider on each side; it was probably cut down for it to hang in a narrower space. This has reduced the impact of the globe and rendered unintelligible the poem in praise of Elizabeth.

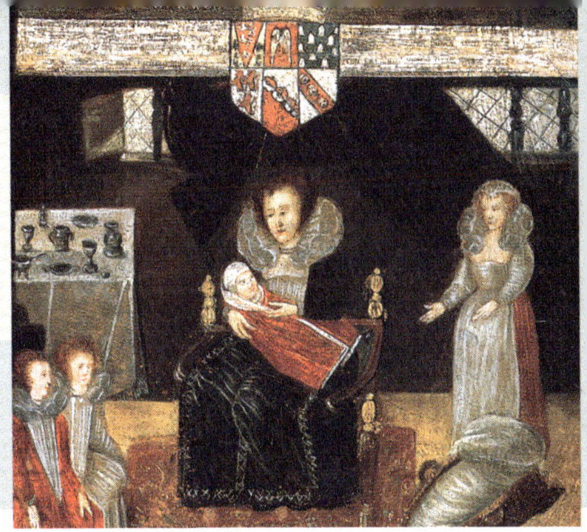

Sir Henry Unton
(Detail of Sir Henry as a baby with his mother, Anne, Countess of Warwick)

Henry Unton's life (1557?–96) is a tale of turning difficulties into successes. Born a second son, after leaving university Unton travelled in Italy perfecting his languages – Venice and Padua appear in the painting. His older brother, also travelling, was imprisoned by the Inquisition and Henry honed his diplomatic skills in England, France and Italy in getting him released, though soon afterwards he died, leaving Henry as heir. A spell fighting in the Low Countries under his uncle the Earl of Leicester was followed by time back at home and in parliament. In the 1590s Unton was sent twice as ambassador to the King of France.

Though an honour to serve the queen, whose miniature portrait he wears around his neck in the painting, it was also a dubious task – she failed to pay the cost of his embassies and was often critical. However, when he lay ill in France she was most concerned. So was the French King, who sent his own doctor, shown in the painting taking Henry's pulse, and visited Unton himself. As Unton had died in her service, when Henry's body was returned to England Elizabeth allowed him the burial of a baron, two ranks above his usual status and almost at the level of his mother the countess. This explains the large amount of space devoted to the funeral procession in the memorial picture.

Henry Unton's mother, Anne, Countess of Warwick (1538–87) was, either by birth or marriage, related to many of the people in this book. Among this illustrious cast were two of Henry VIII's queens, Jane Seymour and Catherine Parr, Jane's son Edward VI and both of his Lords Protector, as well as Elizabeth's favourite, the Earl of Leicester. However, her high status mainly brought Anne immense pain. She was, unfortunately, also related to Lady Jane Grey and suffered the wrath of Mary I after Jane's nine days as queen. Anne, having been widowed by Mary, decided to disappear from public life. She sought obscurity by choosing as her second husband an ordinary Berkshire gentleman, who does not appear anywhere in the Unton painting. Anne's mental state remained fragile and by 1582 she was declared 'of unsound mind'. For her son Henry, his mother's social connections were essential in advancing his career; his life was dedicated to rising to her former high status.

Sir Henry Unton
Unknown artist,
c. 1596

The painting was commissioned by Dorothy, Lady Unton (*died* 1634) after her husband's death in 1596. Reading from the bottom right in an anti-clockwise direction across the top of the painting to his portrait, you can see Unton's babyhood, his time studying at Oxford, his trip to Italy, his military service in the Low Countries and his embassy to France, culminating in his deathbed, with death shown as a skeleton. These different scenes from his life surround a banquet at his Berkshire home, with musicians and dancers performing a masque based on classical themes. The remainder of the picture, to the left of his portrait, shows his coffined body being returned from France, the funeral procession to Faringdon Church, the burial sermon in progress and his monument (in reality placed inside the church) displaying the marble figures of himself and Dorothy.

The painting does not attempt to depict real space: the geography of Europe is telescoped, while the Alps are represented by just four peaks. Each time Henry Unton appears in a scene he is far larger than the people around him and, despite the passage of several decades in the events shown, they are all depicted in the costume of the late 1590s.

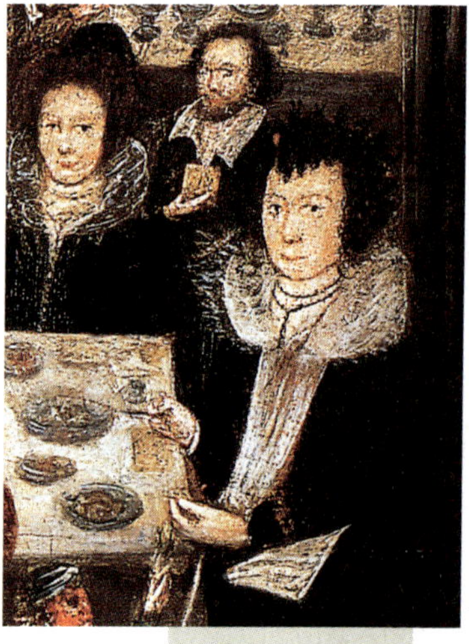

Sir Henry Unton
(Detail of Dorothy, Lady Unton, on the right)

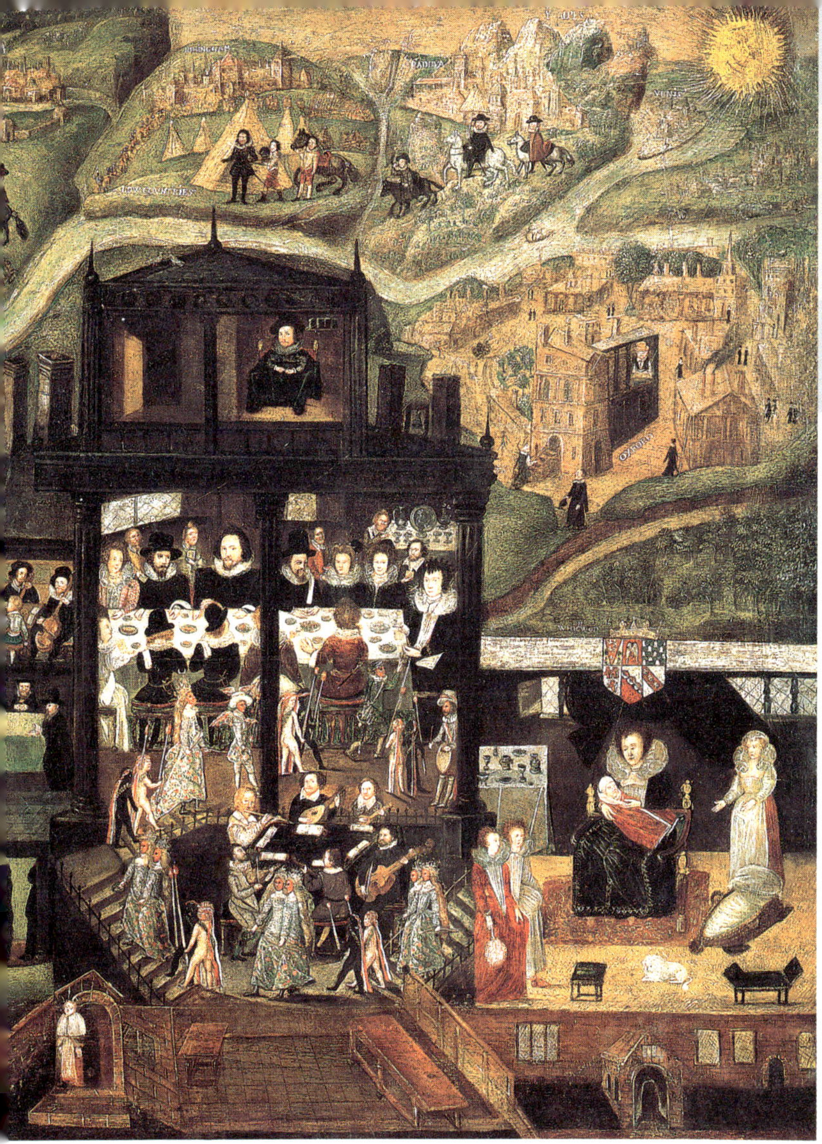
LOW COUNTRIES
Y ALPES
VENIS
OXFORD

Sir Henry Unton
(Detail of Fame)

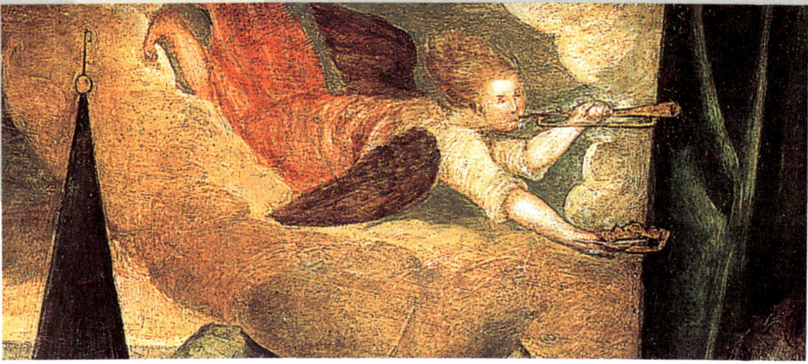

The picture has strong symbolic content. The English Channel, which runs from East to West across the painting, serves also as the River of Life flowing out into the Sea of Eternity. The whole picture is divided into two unequal parts, with life to the East and death, the larger section, to the West. However, there is symmetry in the symbols: the sun and the moon in the corners; the skeleton and the winged figure of Fame; and the doves of peace balancing the ravens of death to either side of the large portrait of Unton.

The winged figure of Fame, carrying her trumpet, hastens to crown Unton's achievements with a wreath. Fame certainly crowned many of the Tudor men and women who appear in this book. Their magnificent portraits displayed in the National Portrait Gallery help to keep their memories alive. However, these fascinating images still harbour some remaining mysteries, and offer continuing scope for new discoveries and interpretations.